TOOLS
FOR A SUCCESSFUL
LiFE

Willie Gilchrist, EdD

Book design by www.arborbooks.com

Printed in the United States

Tools for a Successful Life
Willie Gilchrist, EdD

1. Title 2. Author 3. Self-help

Library of Congress Control Number: 2014915931

ISBN: 978-0-692-28713-2

To my wife, Jacqueline, and our children:
Wyvondalynn and her husband, Nathan;
Steven and his wife, T'sha;
Willie II and his fiancée, Bailee.

TABLE OF CONTENTS

INTRODUCTION

My life has not always been filled with sunshine and crisp, clear, beautiful skies. I have surely seen my share of dark clouds and survived some raging thunderstorms. But then, who hasn't? We all have our trials and our triumphs, our dim and bright times, the days we hope will quickly end and those we wish could last for all eternity. This is part of the human experience, a shared reality that binds us all together in the end.

Still, each of us has a unique story to tell. Beneath the surfaces of our lives, the fundamental elements of our beings form in countless different ways, making us who we are. In this book I will share my story because I believe it might shed light on some overarching truths. First, that people are inherently good; it's just the nature of humans to get sidetracked sometimes. Second, that we reap what we sow, a lesson my parents taught me as a child. This means that if we put in the necessary work and base our decisions on sound, strong morals, our results will be consistently positive and in line with our desires. It also means we must invest in ourselves—and, later in life, our children and grandchildren—emotionally, spiritually, and financially in order to create good outcomes in the future.

Perhaps these ideas don't sound entirely new to you. Surely others have thought them before, culled from their own experiences. But that's the circle of life, isn't it? We learn from one another. By watching what those around us do and the consequences of their actions, we see what we should and should not do ourselves. We learn the tools we need to get us through this life and navigate our world. Thus great notions are recycled and revived from generation to generation. It's like what happens in our popular culture, where trends in clothes and music go out of style then come back again a couple decades later. I've seen it happen so many times throughout my life, and I'm not talking just about bell-bottom jeans or an updated cover of a "golden oldies" song. No, what I mean here is an essential truth: each of us is part of the big picture of life just as our parents were and their parents before them, ad infinitum.

Some things never change, and that fact is one of them whether you're a teenager, a young adult, or retired like me. Every lesson, every tool for living I discuss in this book has applied to me at each developmental stage in my life, and I am sure you'll find something relevant to your situation in them too. What lessons could a man like me have to teach? Well, they're simple:

It's human nature to doubt our own talents and skills, but don't let that govern your actions.

We all think we're smarter than our parents at some point—but we're not.

Working hard—that is, putting your all into everything you do, body, mind, and soul—is the key to creating the life you want to live.

Education is extremely important. Learning is a continual, lifelong process that does not begin nor end in the classroom. Life itself is the best teacher you will ever have.

No one's journey is simple. There are potholes in every road.

And no one can travel that path alone. We all need our support systems if we want to find success, which is as individual as our fingerprints. What I consider success will be different from your definition, and neither is less valid than the other. It's all in the eye of the beholder.

Whoever you are, whatever you're striving toward—whether it's earning a college degree, landing a better job, or simply finding happiness and peace in your life—take comfort in the fact that you're not alone. I have been where you are, as have many people before us. We all have struggled and sweated to make our lives the best they can be and then to pass that wealth we've earned, be it intellectual or monetary, down to our children. To leave legacies of which we can be proud. No matter what our fields of work or interest, this is at the root of all we do: the compulsion to transform ourselves (and, by association, the ones we love) into the best versions of ourselves that we can be.

In the end you are in control of your destiny. You *can* work hard, persevere, and get what you want. Maybe not today, maybe not tomorrow or even next month or next year. Some dreams take lifetimes to fulfill. But that does not mean you should ever stop trying. If you give up, you get nothing; if you keep on despite whatever difficulties you might face, then you will realize your goal. The only person responsible for your success or failure in all things is you; do not allow anyone else to take on that duty. Create the best future for yourself and those you love by having a good work ethic, staying focused, always remaining loyal, and putting forth your best effort on a daily basis.

I can tell, from the fact that you're reading this book, that you are ready to take on this challenge as well. So go get your toolbox, and we'll begin.

Don't Let Difficult Circumstances Hold You Back

By all rights I should have given up the fight long ago. When I was just a kid actually. There were just too many factors working against me. I was the middle child of six born to blue-collar parents, and though we were poor, I didn't know it because no one ever told me as much. In my childlike view of the world, I was worth just as much as those people across town who lived in the big mansions, the ones with the view of the Atlantic Ocean. Our backyard was the size of a postage stamp, and there were three bedrooms to split among us all.

We lived in Florida then, where both my parents had agricultural jobs. Dad did seasonal work picking oranges, Mom with celery and cabbages. All of it was backbreaking, but I didn't know that either because my parents never let their pain show. Sure, I heard them moan about their aching knees and blistered hands from time to time, and they always seemed exhausted. But that never stopped them from taking care of my siblings and me. Quite the opposite, it made them work harder so they could provide us with better than they had.

That is the dream of any competent, caring parent, isn't it? We want our children to surpass us. No matter how successful we are, we know they can do something better, greater. And it is our responsibility to set them up for that, to give them access to all the opportunities that exist for them. We must ensure they have not just good but exceptional educations from the time they are young. We must encourage them to earn college degrees and help them to do so financially as much as we can. If they need a place to live for a while in order to save money, our doors are always open. Just because they've reached the age of majority, that doesn't mean we can't still take care of them as they need. A strong support system is so important—but we'll get to that topic later.

At any rate, I understand this is not possible for all people, especially the financial part. Not all parents have high-paying jobs or access to the best schools. This was certainly the case as I was coming up. My parents worked long hours for little pay, and most of it went simply to maintaining our life: bills and rent, food on the table, and that was that. We existed in a constant state of what you might call *getting by*.

And that, after a while, was just not good enough for Mom and Dad. Yes, they supported their family, but it was not enough. They wanted—again, as all parents do—for my siblings and me to have better lives, to have childhoods as free of worry as possible so we might grow into positive-minded and ambitious adults without the psychological baggage so many people end up saddled with as they grow. This meant we needed more money, more food security, and a safer place to live. Which meant they had to get different jobs, ones that paid higher wages and hopefully took much less toll on their bodies.

Unfortunately that kind of work didn't exist in Florida at the time, at least not in the region where we lived. But my parents did not let that stop them. It was a hurdle, for sure, but one they were willing to jump if it meant they could better provide for their family. And the leap they took was a big one—all the way to Rochester, New York, which was experiencing a bit of a boom in the mid-1950s. Many people were moving into the city, so there were roads to be built, houses to be raised, and so on. Jobs were plentiful and, from what my parents heard, paying extremely well. So that was where they looked. They did not want to be away from their children, but this was an opportunity for them to earn higher pay, to build up their family strong, and, also important, to get out of the fields.

My dad was snapped up quickly for a construction job in New York, and my mom found employment as a domestic worker. This was in the spring, and they would stay in Rochester until the end of fall, when the building jobs started to taper off. They left me and the other younger children in the care of our sixteen-year-old sister and our grandmother, who lived next door. It was not an ideal situation by any stretch of the imagination, but it was my parents' best choice. This was how they could make life better for our family.

I was only eight then, so I did not fully understand that.

I mostly knew my parents were gone much of the time, and I missed them, though I did have my siblings to keep me company—especially my older brother, Johnny. He was the closest to me in age, and perhaps that was why we spent so much time together just by default. But over and above that, I looked up to him. He was my older brother, after all. And in an odd way, I think he revered me a little bit too.

"Say hello to my bookworm brother," he would always say as a means of introduction then he'd side-eye me and shoot me a sly grin because what he'd said was in no way an insult. In fact it was the truth; I did love to read then just as much as I do now. And my parents encouraged that. They saw something in me, I suppose, that let them know I would be able to make something of myself despite our less than perfect circumstances. That I would eventually rise above. So they pushed me hard not just in reading but in all areas of my life.

That's not to say, though, that they imposed their own dreams onto me. I suppose they had not always aspired to work in the hot sun, picking fruits and vegetables, or in construction or as a domestic employee. These were hard jobs; they were labor in the truest sense of the word. And they certainly had not ever thought they would end up so far away from their children just so they could—ironically—provide us with better lives than they had. Given their difficult circumstances, it would have been easy for them to put the burden of all their lost dreams on my siblings and me, but they did not do that. Instead they developed in each of us, and particularly in me, the sense of being an independent thinker. They would provide as much means for us to succeed as they could, but in the end the choice of what to do with that help was up to us.

This, in my opinion, is one of the most important jobs a parent can do. When we encourage our children to aim for success in something about which they feel passionate, we in essence give them wings. We don't saddle them down with what *we* want them to do, and in the process we show them that we trust them to make good choices for themselves. Of course we give them guidance, little nudges in the directions we think will benefit them the most. But at the end of the day, they are rational, thinking human beings just like we are, and they are going to do what they want to do.

Of course at that young an age—remember, I was eight when my parents began working in Rochester—I didn't understand this concept as I do now. I saw my parents working hard, but I did not know the extent of their sacrifices for my siblings and me. They were survivors and providers, overcoming great adversity in order to fulfill what was really their dream: to have a big, happy, healthy family full of children who grew up to do great things with their lives. I think—I hope—that I have fulfilled that for them.

Keep Your Eyes Open

When you're down and out, it can be hard to imagine yourself any other way. You're working eighty hours a week just to get by; you're so entrenched in responsibilities that you barely have time to spend with your family, and when you do, you're always stressed out anyway and don't enjoy it—and neither do they. So many people live this way day in and day out. Sometimes it is unavoidable. And that sort of existence can wear even the strongest souls down.

However, those brave hearts also know that they cannot let their current problems hold them back. They might be trudging through life at the moment, but at least they are moving—albeit slowly—toward something. Maybe they can't see what it is yet, but the goal is out there, just like the proverbial light at the end of the tunnel. And more likely than not, that light is a ray of sunshine, not a train barreling down on them.

I hear so many people these days say that poverty is inescapable—that if you grow up poor, you are destined to be poor your whole life. For some this is true and often through no fault of their own. There are myriad social, cultural, and legal factors in this great nation of ours that work to keep much of our underprivileged classes down. However, I am here to tell you: it's at least *possible*. You *can* improve your station in life. It's not going to be easy, but the opportunity at least is out there for you. If you had no money growing up, you *can* eventually become financially successful. If you have a physical disability, you *can* adapt your environment to fit the way in which you want to live. If you lack education, you *can* still go back to school and earn that degree you've always wanted, no matter how old you are.

What I'm saying here is another adage that probably will

not be new to your eyes: where there's a will, there's a way. If you *want* to do it, you *can* do it. That's not a guarantee of success but an acknowledgment that achieving your goals is *possible* if you work hard and, as they say, keep your eyes on the prize. With little more than determination and focus, many people have accomplished miraculous transformations in themselves and their lives.

Although, there is one more factor that must be in the mix as well: patience. Especially in today's world, and especially among the younger generations, everybody wants everything now, now, *now*! We live in a technology-driven world where practically all existing information is at our fingertips via our smartphones. Just twenty years ago, if you wanted to know, say, what the capital of Bulgaria is or how many centimeters are in a mile, you would have to go to the library to look it up. And there were no computer databases there either, just the big, old card catalogs and the Dewey Decimal System. Finding out such minute bits of information could take hours, if not days.

Now knowledge can come to us almost instantaneously, and so we have become inpatient. We want what we want when we want it, and we do not want to wait. Most of the time there's no reason to. Except, of course, when it comes to planning out your life and how you are going to reach your goals. This is not something that can be rushed, especially when you finally begin to enact those plans. Some dreams might be realized overnight, but more often than not it's going to take you a good long while. You'll get there; you just have to have patience and trust that if you stay on the right path, good things will come in time.

First Things First

Unfortunately I have not always taken my own good advice. When I was younger, when I was just starting out in life, I thought I could do everything at once. I was married by the time I graduated from college; I earned a master's degree while working full time as a teacher. Then I got the bright idea to pursue an EdD—a doctor of education degree—so I could enter into the field of school administration.

That seems like a good plan on the surface. It sounds like I was following the right path. And in the beginning I thought I was. However, at the time, my wife, Jacqueline, and I had three small children, and she was working full time as well. So was I, plus going to school at nights, so most of the childrearing responsibilities fell to her. Talk about burning the candle at both ends—ours, I think, was on fire from the middle too.

It took me a while to realize this. But when I did, it hit me like a ton of bricks. *What am I doing?* I wondered. I barely saw my wife and kids, and I was exhausted all the time, so when I was home, all I wanted to do was sleep. My days lasted from six in the morning until ten at night sometimes, long after the children were in bed. I could go a week sometimes without seeing them.

And that did not sit right with me. In fact it bothered me a lot. I didn't have a family so I could ignore them in pursuit of my own goals. Yes, I wanted an EdD so I could get a better job, which ultimately would benefit all of us thanks to the increased pay. But at what price? Were a fatter paycheck and more esteem from my peers worth losing my family for? Was this degree so important that I had to have it right at that moment—and risk not seeing my children as they grew up?

I'm sure you can guess the answers to those questions. They are not hard to figure out. So I brought the issue to Jacqueline, and we discussed it then made a decision together: It wasn't that I wanted to be home more because I didn't trust her to care for our growing family. Quite the contrary, she was—and is—the best mother I ever could have wanted my children to have. I just wanted to be there to enjoy that time with her. So we decided I would take a break from working on my doctorate, maintain my full-time job, and focus on building our strong family structure. Nothing was more important than that. And once I realized this, I saw the selfishness of my ways, and I knew I could do better. But I had to sacrifice what I wanted for the greater good, at least for a little while, and put my family first. Everything else after that would come in time.

So how did that situation work out? Well, Jacqueline and I have been married for forty-two years now, and our children are all grown. They've earned multiple degrees and have pursued careers in business management (and then a second career in nursing) and computer science and as a medical doctor. So I'd say it went just fine.

A Challenge Is an Opportunity in Disguise

I eventually did get my EdD, and I did go into school administration as a principal. But I didn't let my dreams stop there. I had my eye on a superintendent position within the school district where I had worked for seventeen years, and I decided to throw my hat in the ring, so to speak. I approached the chair of the board of education and let him know about my interest.

And right away he shot me down. "We've already tried out a couple African-American superintendents," he told me. "It's time to try a Caucasian."

I could not believe my ears. Was he really telling me outright that I could not get the position because I was African-American? Granted, this was back in the 1980s, when people felt freer to make openly racist comments than they do today. I walked away from that conversation with my head literally hanging, with my chin touching my chest. However, this was not out of shame. No, I wasn't embarrassed by what he said; his words did not make me feel bad about myself or my race. I was simply thinking about what to do from there. Should I have made a case out of it? I could have reported the chairman to a higher authority, maybe even gotten him kicked off the board if I tried.

But what would that have solved? It might have made me feel better in the short term, having enacted my revenge. But it would not win me that superintendent position I wanted. So instead of reacting how I imagined this little man had wanted me to, I picked my head up again and held it high. I said a short prayer, and then I just kept going. I was not about to let anyone shatter my dreams, in particular not this guy. And I try not to hold grudges because all they do is hold us back. "Vengeance is mine," says the Bible. I stayed focused on the prize. I knew my time would come.

A short while after that, the board of education—comprised of three Caucasians and four African-Americans—did indeed bring in a white superintendent. A man named Chuck. I worked under him, and he seemed like a nice and competent enough guy. We didn't have too much contact but enough to know we got along all right.

So it was a surprise when Chuck paid me a visit one day and asked to talk in my office.

"Willie," he said, sitting on the other side of my desk. He paused as if trying to figure out what he wanted to say. "It's no secret that you're well liked around here."

I laughed a little. As a principal I had made it my mandate to stay as involved as possible with both students and teachers, to motivate all of them to do the best they could and to assist them in that endeavor however I could. "You could say that," I acquiesced.

The superintendent cleared his throat. All of a sudden his face looked very serious. "Well, Willie," he went on, "let's just say that's not exactly a good thing right now."

I looked at him blankly, unsure what he was trying to imply. Was this another racist statement, albeit a little more veiled than the chairman's had been?

"I don't understand," I said, hoping it would nudge him to continue.

It did. "All I'm saying is you're too popular. Not just in your school but around the entire district. Everyone knows about you, Willie, and they can't get enough. People talk about you and the methods you use to run your school and all these great practices you've instituted."

That made me grin. I'm not an overly proud man by nature, but I had certainly made some achievements during my principalship, and it was nice to hear they were appreciated.

"It's too much," Chuck went on, his voice dropping lower, sounding almost apologetic. He even shook his head a little. "I know you don't mean to do it, Willie, but you're undermining my authority. I can't get things done when people keep comparing me to the great Willie Gilchrist."

I brought my hand up to my mouth, stifling a laugh. "Okay, Chuck," I said, trying to keep my voice calm. "So what's the point here? What do you want me to do?"

He sighed and sat back. "My idea is that you should come and be my associate superintendent."

My stomach lurched a little at these words and not entirely in a good way. Why was he offering this? So he could keep tabs on me? That was my first thought, and immediately it did not sit right with me.

"Well, I don't know about that," I said, shifting uncomfortably in my chair. "I'm pretty settled here, and I—"

"Willie," Chuck interrupted, holding up a hand to cut me off. "I'm not asking. I'm telling. Either you accept the position as associate superintendent, or I'm going to transfer you to the other high school in the district. I have to break up whatever hold you have on this place. It's becoming distracting, not just here but even in other schools."

So it was a threat, not a request. And I knew right away I had no choice. I couldn't leave this school. I had been there for seventeen years; it was everything I knew. Going to another school and starting all over again would have been, in my estimation, a step back.

"Well, since you put it that way," I said, trying to keep a convincing smile on my face.

Within the month I was reporting for duty at my new post as associate superintendent for the Northampton County school district in North Carolina. And I found, surprisingly, it wasn't as bad as I'd expected it to be. Though Chuck could be blunt, and I wasn't crazy about how he had gotten me into this position, he was an excellent teacher. He brought me onboard and up to speed right away, and not once did he speak down to me or give me busy work. I was an integral part of the superintendent team, as it were, and Chuck was my mentor. I was very lucky and blessed—not to mention elated—that he had so much confidence in me.

In fact he believed in my skills and talents so much that just three months into this new job, he hit me with another revelation. We were in his office, door closed, just talking about the usual district business. At one point he just stopped and looked at me.

"You know," he said, "you should be sitting behind this desk, not me, Willie."

I was floored. Why would he say that? I mean, sure, I agreed with him; I had wanted the superintendent position long before he'd been hired. But that had not been in the cards for me at the time, and Chuck had been a good choice on the board's part. He was dedicated and talented and filled the seat very well as far as I was concerned.

"The board just picked me and put me here." He looked at me again, waiting for a response. But I had none. So he continued. "It was a political move. You know how they are."

Indeed I did. Chuck was Caucasian, and that was why the board had given him this job, just as the chairman had said they would. Even Chuck admitted it now. Did that change the fact that he was good at what he did? No, of course not. Did it change the fact that I was the associate superintendent instead of the man in charge?

No. In fact it changed nothing. But Chuck's acknowledgment did let me know that he was being honest with me, that he valued me enough to give me that courtesy. He also told me that I would be a superintendent myself one day, he was sure of it, and gave me some pointers that might get me there a little more quickly. Chuck never did anything but motivate and encourage me, and I gained great hands-on experience working with him. I did assume the role of superintendent just eight months later, in neighboring Halifax County, and I am sure I would have bombed out if it hadn't been for Chuck's steady guidance.

As you might imagine, my appointment to this new position was quite controversial. The members of the board of education were all the same as last time—three Caucasians and four African-Americans—and this time the latter all voted in my favor. Displeased with that outcome, the other three then tried to stonewall me when it came time to negotiate, probably thinking they could discourage me from taking the job if they made it look bad enough. And they surely did. The salary they offered was way below what I was looking for—low enough that walking away at that point would have been smart.

However, I have never been one to slink away from a challenge. They wanted to play hardball? *So be it,* I thought. We went back and forth a few times, each of us throwing out numbers that didn't make much difference one way or the other. Finally it became clear: they were not going to budge, and I could take it or leave it. So to everyone's surprise—even my own, to tell the truth—I took it. I ended the bargaining and simply assumed my role as superintendent of the school district.

Well, that just made my detractors even more furious, and they did all they could to make my working life a living hell. Within my first month on the job, one of the African-Americans on the board died suddenly, leaving only six members. They never did add another seventh person, which is essential when it comes to voting on proposals and requests. Without that tiebreaker, the board was constantly at a stalemate—particularly when the request was mine. I could not get them to agree on any major issues that I needed to address, and very little I proposed was ever passed.

Things went on in this fashion for my first two years as superintendent. Aside from the voting problem, the board was always looking over my shoulder, monitoring my work and acting suspicious of everything I did. It got so bad that I even began to doubt myself. Had I made the right decision in taking this job? Some days I wondered. But most of the time, I tried not to let their negativity drag me down. I had work to do and people for whom I was responsible, both staff and students. That was first and foremost in my mind.

Eventually the deceased board member was replaced—by his widow, bringing the makeup of the committee back to four African-Americans and three Caucasians. Not long after that, one of the latter was hit by a car and passed away, but she was one of the few who had been on my side, so of course I was grieved she was no longer around. Then at the next election, the worst of my three detractors was voted out, and that was the point when things began looking up. In fact they got downright good. For the next ten years, the board members and I worked together to lead the district. They didn't approve of every idea I brought before them, and we still had our clashes. But on the whole they understood their roles, and I understood mine, and we didn't cross each other's paths. At last I had the freedom to perform my work as I saw fit without the constant scrutiny, and I settled into the job and never looked back, not once in the next ten years that I held the position.

Education Is Key

"I was the first person in my family to go to college."

How many times have you heard this sentence? It's a common phenomenon—a person of a younger generation beating the odds, whatever they may be, and applying to, being accepted by, and attending a university to pursue a higher degree of education. Every year in the United States, about 30 percent of all college enrollees fall within this "first generation" category, which can be a source of immense pride for both the student and his or her family, but it can also cause an enormous amount of stress. Being first means no one before them had a college education, and that means there are no role models for the young person to follow when trying to figure out what to do. The first-generation student, then, is often like a sailboat adrift in a very large sea.

This becomes even more difficult when the young person in question is the son or daughter of immigrants (the first generation of the family born in this country) or economically disadvantaged, though the two often go hand in hand. Students from these demographic groups are more likely to delay applying for and enrolling in college; when they do finally matriculate, they enter the academic arena much less prepared than their peers and are four times more likely to drop out after the first year.

Why does this happen? Because often their parents are not college educated themselves and lack the necessary knowledge to assist their children with applications and financial concerns. Because the parents have spent their adult lives—and, in many cases, much of their childhoods—working to support themselves and their families, including parents and brothers and sisters. Whereas parents who did receive college educations are likely to see higher learning as an extension of their children's academic and social experiences, the immigrant or low-income families are often not even aware that attending a university is a choice.

This was a trap I could have fallen into easily with my own family. My parents had not gone to college; in fact they had been forced to abandon their schooling early on due to family circumstances. Mom got to the seventh grade, and Dad never made it past grade five. This did not mean they were lacking intelligence; just the opposite, they were two of the smartest people I have known.

But without that formal education, without those degrees to hang on the wall, their lives were difficult—much more so than they would have been otherwise. They struggled to find jobs at times, and when they did get work it was generally intense, backbreaking labor. Even if they had wanted to finish their schooling at some point later in their lives, I doubt they would have had the time or the physical energy to go through with it.

However, that was okay with them. They had all the things they had wanted in their lives—they had each other and their children, and somehow that made everything they had to do to support us a little less harrowing. But it also meant that when it came time for me to think about going to college, basically I was on my own. My parents, though they had always encouraged me to take my education seriously and were fully behind my desire to go study at a university, nonetheless had no idea how the entire process worked. Which schools were good for which majors? What was I supposed to write for my application essay? Should we visit campuses? Would financial aid be available to me?

This, then, is the difference for someone who's the first in their family to go to college or even to want to go. There were a thousand questions I needed answered, and unfortunately my parents could not help me much. They wanted me to go to school. I don't know how many times in my life they had told me they didn't want me to end up like they had. They worked so hard, and what did they have to show for it? As I've said before, we were just getting by. When I grew older and came closer to graduating from high school and ostensibly becoming an adult, I understood this more and more. And I did not want that sort of life. Nor did they want it for me.

That was why, when I contemplated skipping college to

join the construction crew with my dad, he told me in a very stern, commanding voice: "Son, I don't want you out there in the blazing sun and bitter cold. I don't want you to work beside me. Don't follow in my footsteps."

Those are heavy words for a child to hear from his parent. Because no matter if you're wealthy or poor, if your parents take good care of you, won't you look up to them? You'll see nothing shameful in what they do to put food on the table, to keep a roof over your head. And this was how I viewed my mom and dad. They each had an amazing work ethic, and I admired that so much about them. They toiled so many hours a day and traveled long distances to support my siblings and me, and they did it without complaint. Again, as I got older I appreciated the sacrifices they made for us—for me. So when they told me not to end up like them, I couldn't help but feel a little torn.

Plus there was the issue of money. My father was paid well in the construction trade, and if I worked with him, I would most likely do the same. I wouldn't start at his level, of course, but I would be diligent and work my way up. As a young man who was just starting out in the world, I found the idea of having a little in cash in my pocket to be quite enticing. If I went to college, I might work part time, but the majority of my life would be devoted to my studies, and any money I earned would likely go toward supplies or room and board. That meant at least four more years of just getting by financially, whereas if I worked with my dad, I could start earning (and spending and saving) right away. And, though of course I didn't know it at the time, if I took that opportunity I would not have met Jacqueline and surely would not have been blessed with Wyvondalynn, Steven, and Willie II.

So you can see my dilemma. One of my brothers felt this way too. He could have gone to college if he wanted to; it wasn't as though my parents encouraged only me in this pursuit. Any one of us, if we applied ourselves to it, could have gotten into a university and worked toward whatever degree we envisioned. But my brother couldn't handle the delayed gratification. He wanted to make money right away, to help him get on with his life—to find his own place to live and someday start a family of his own.

I wanted these things too. Independence and a wife and kids were certainly in my future. But when I was eighteen years old, I could not even see that point on the horizon. I was all about me then—what teenager isn't?—and what would be best for me. So for the time being, I decided I was willing to postpone my fortune in order to pursue a higher education. I would go to college.

⁓

Later in life, after I earned my EdD and entered into school administration, I remembered my younger days and the clamoring I had done while trying to figure out just what this college thing was all about. As I've said, my parents didn't know too much about it, and surprisingly neither did my counselors at school. Perhaps it was the area in which we lived, but they were more interested in telling kids like me to look into the blue-collar sector, to get a job at a factory or in auto repair or any number of hands-on trades. There were plenty of good jobs, my counselor told me, at Rochester's leading companies—Kodak, General Dynamic, Xerox, General Electric, and Bausch and Lomb—though he meant in their warehouses, not their offices. Knowing my dad worked in construction, the counselor encouraged me to go that way too. But no matter how many times I heard it, I just kept insisting that college was the path for me.

And with that, again, I was left mostly alone. I did all my own research, going to the library and looking up different schools—in state, out of state, anywhere that seemed good. By then I knew I wanted to be a teacher; I'd had a couple good role models along the way who had shown me what a respected profession it could be, and I liked that. I wanted to do something important, something that would help people and bring me some esteem in the process. And I wanted a job where I could wear a suit and tie instead of sitting in the grimy cabin of a backhoe all day. As superficial as that might sound, it was one of my criteria when thinking about careers. Remember, I was coming to all these conclusions on my own.

At the time this was okay to me. I was an independent young man, and I didn't mind working on my own. I enjoyed researching colleges, narrowing down the list, and ultimately deciding on the ones to which I would apply. I wanted to go to a historical black institution, and my counselor told me the best colleges were in North Carolina, New York, and Ohio (the one useful piece of advice he ever gave me). Putting these two factors together, I was able to put Elizabeth City State University in North Carolina at the top of my list. I had never been to the state before except when driving through it on the way from Florida to New York and back, but I liked the feeling of steering my own fate, of finally being able to make decisions about where I would go and what I would do with my life. That's one of the great ironies of being an older teenager and a young adult—you're old enough to make up your own mind about things, but you are still young, so the adults around you tend to make the decisions for you. Sometimes it's helpful, but just as often it can become frustrating.

I tried to keep all this in mind later in my life, when I finally worked in school administration. In my first job as a principal, I became known as a bit of a pusher in the college-application season. I would meet with students individually, sometimes even just stopping them in the hallway to chat about their future goals. Those who wanted to attend college got enthusiastic responses from me, and I did all I could to get them whatever help they needed, from literature about certain schools to information about majors and careers they might enjoy.

For those who expressed no interest in higher education, the ones who would graduate from high school and go into labor jobs like those I mentioned earlier, I had to take a gentler approach. I didn't want to tell them what I thought they should do; this was an important decision, I felt, and one they should come to on their own. But at the same time, I wanted to encourage them as much as possible at least to consider going to college. I wanted them to see their own potential, to understand that even though they did not like the sound of spending another four-plus years in school, in the long run of their lives, the time investment alone would pay them back a thousandfold. I told them about my own experiences as a high-school senior—about how my parents warned me off their lines of work, about how my school counselors did not want to help me. If anyone should have given up on college, it should have been me, I related. But I didn't, and just look where it had gotten me.

If these students remained on the fence, I would bring in their parents and speak to them both in private and with their child to get them onboard with the idea of higher education. Once I had buy-in on that front, it was generally easier to help the kids out. After all, who's as influential in your younger years than your parents?

In addition our school had an excellent, strong, and very involved parent-teacher association, or the PTA. They met regularly to discuss issues not just within the school but in education as a whole. On both sides there were some very insightful people who regularly shared their ideas and opinions and even were able to change some minds on important topics; I knew these were the people I needed on my team in my pro-college campaign. To bolster my mission further, I established an alumni society at the school and invited past graduates to come back for periodic induction ceremonies. This allowed our students to meet people who had gotten out of school, continued their educations, and reached whatever goals they had set out for themselves.

Maybe the kids related to my college story; maybe their moms and dads drilled the need for education into them at home. Perhaps my persistence simply wore them down. Whatever the reason, many of them underwent changes of heart and accepted my offers of help. Together we researched schools and careers and figured out what they really wanted from life.

I did this same routine, all told, for seventeen years, the length of time I worked as a public-school principal. That means I influenced how many students—hundreds? Maybe thousands. I never kept count; my only focus was to help as many as I could, to inspire them to love learning and to place their educations above all other considerations in life. I like to think that in this capacity, I succeeded more often than I didn't.

And I didn't stop my efforts with the students. No, learning is a lifelong pursuit, not something you do as a young person then abandon once you're an adult. Especially in the education field, we must continually update our knowledge and skills; we must strive to know more than we did yesterday while looking to the future, toward what we want to know tomorrow. This mindset of curiosity and drive are what make great teachers and great school administrators. They were the qualities I tried to exemplify in my work—and instill in my staff.

Toward this end I was always on the lookout for teachers with that little something extra, the spark that made the students really respond to what they did in their classrooms.

Maybe they were exceptional speakers or had innovative ways of conveying difficult topics. Maybe they were compassionate listeners and really showed the kids that they cared about them as human beings, not just test grades on paper.

Whatever these teachers' special talents were, I noted them both to myself and to the teachers, and I encouraged them to take it further—along with their careers. Just as I did with the students, I helped some teachers pursue additional higher education, whether they wanted EdDs or another master's or whatever would help them teach better or, if they wanted to, move up in the ranks. In this way I motivated at least nine teachers I can think of, over my seventeen years as a principal, to go into school administration.

I was pretty proud of this achievement, and even when I advanced to the role of superintendent, I kept it in the back of my mind. Now that I was in a position with a little more power and responsibility, I wondered how I could help the teachers in my district even more than I already had. This wasn't about me, of course; I wasn't looking for some sort of praise or glory. I merely had seen the success I'd motivated people to achieve as a principal, and now, I felt, I was in a place where I could take it to another level. I could bring opportunities to those who might not otherwise have access to them.

This opportunity knocked when as superintendent, I was appointed by the governor of North Carolina to be the cochair of a statewide educational task force. This increased my reach considerably; I now had the ears of not just the other administrators in my district but those at other schools in other counties. I even had access to some college-level personnel, and that got me thinking: what if I could not just motivate my district's teachers to pursue further degrees but actually give them the means to do it? Not monetarily—it would have been nice to pay for all their educations, but that would have taken a real dream budget to achieve. Instead, what I could offer was access to the college courses they would need to take.

With this in mind I approached the School of Education at East Carolina University with a proposal: I wanted them to work with me to develop a program wherein my teachers could earn master's degrees in school administration. It took a bit of finagling on my part—they were interested in the idea but of course wanted to map out all the logistics first. And in the end we came up with a comprehensive offering tailored specifically to already-working teachers who wanted to pursue such degrees. Once we opened it up, the response was overwhelming—fifty-nine of the teachers in my district enrolled, and fifty-six graduated with degrees in administration. I have to say I was proud of this accomplishment at the time, and I still am because I believe now just as I did back then: education truly is the key. It can unlock doors you don't even know exist right now to pathways that you might never have considered taking. No matter who you are, where you are from, or how much money you have, don't let any of that stop you. Go to college. Get your degree. And watch the world open up for you.

Work Hard

There's an old saying that goes something like this: do what you love, and you'll never work a day in your life. Meaning that when you pursue a career that fulfills you not just professionally but on a personal level, it will not seem like a job at all but a calling. You'll look forward to getting up in the mornings and heading to your office, your clinic, your school, or wherever it is you spend your forty (or probably more) hours per week. You'll approach each task with enthusiasm and diligence and take pride in the positive outcomes that result. Most of all you will share this love for what you do with everyone around you through your words and actions, thus inspiring them to do their best as well. This sort of passion, you could say, can be contagious—but in a good way. It's the kind of bug you want to catch.

Maybe this all sounds quite cliché. To some it might sound downright impossible. For so many people in this country, and indeed around the world, work and pleasure are mutually exclusive. They can't imagine the two ever intersecting. A job is simply a way to earn a paycheck for those who think this way; they drag themselves into their workplaces, put in the bare minimum expected of them then trudge home again at night feeling as if they've accomplished nothing that day or, sadly, throughout their lives. It's an endless cycle that serves only to drain the worker's energy and, in truth, his or her joy. Work life and home life are just that intimately interconnected—when one suffers, the other usually follows suit.

Though I initially decided to become a teacher because I wanted to wear nice suits and feel as though people looked up to me, once I got to working in the field, I found there was so much more to the experience than that. I say *experience*, not *job*, because that's what teaching and administrating has been for me. It's more than what I do to get paid so I can support my family and myself; it's an ongoing lesson in perseverance, creativity, and so much more. My career has become an expression of who I am as a person—my values, my beliefs, and my philosophies on life, all of which I honed over the years I spent in education.

I know how fortunate this makes me. I fully recognize and appreciate that not everyone can feel this way about his or her work. For some a job must be that means to the end, the factor that keeps the roof over their heads and dinner on the table. Passion and fulfillment do not even enter into the picture out of necessity, for they are nothing but distractions in such cases.

The money is the important thing, not how the work makes them feel on an existential level.

This, as we have discussed, was where my parents found themselves time and time again. Whether they were picking oranges and celery and cabbage in the hot, dirty farmlands of Florida or driving backhoes and washing other people's laundry up in New York, the work they did was just that: work. They did not find personal satisfaction in it. Construction and domestic care did not really challenge them intellectually, and so they approached them at face value—as ways to earn money for buying food and paying bills. Nothing more, nothing less. That was all there was to it.

Still, that does not mean my parents did not give their all in the jobs they performed. If you're going to work, my father always told me, do your best. Don't cut corners. Don't try to push your responsibilities off onto someone else. If you're getting a full day's pay then put in a full day's work. Earn what you earn. And most of all, be honest—that's what it comes down to in the end.

This was his work ethic, or the set of values he applied in any position he held. My father passed this mindset down to me not just through his example but also in words.

"Never show up at a jobsite with the intention of being lazy or slacking off," he would tell me even when I was quite young, before I could understand completely the sacrifices he and Mom were making for our family. "When you're on the clock, stay busy at all times. If you run out of tasks, find more. There's always something that needs to be done or attended to, and everything you do helps the place where you work advance. When it does, you will progress as well. It's a win-win situation, and it's in your power to make it happen."

Of course I took his advice to heart—simply because I heeded everything my father said. He might not have had a college degree or even a high-school diploma, but he was one of the wisest people I have ever known, and when he spoke, I took note. And thank goodness I did in this case because those lessons are what propelled me through my working life. Without Dad's advice, without that work ethic he taught me, I probably would not have achieved half the things I've managed to do in my life. In fact I'm sure of it, and I know that over the years, I made him proud.

As I've mentioned before, wanting the best for our children—or at least better than we had—is a hallmark of good parenting. Toward that end my wife and I have worked hard to raise our children with the same work ethic my father instilled in me when I was a boy. As far as I'm concerned, a child is never too young to begin to learn personal accountability; even a toddler can understand that if he takes out all his toys, when he's through playing, he must return them to their rightful places. Such lessons can seem small or even trivial, but, on the contrary, they are vitally important. That sense of responsibility learned early on will translate later in life as professional responsibility as well.

The work I have pursued throughout my life has been very different from the jobs my parents took in order to keep our family going. I have had the privilege to choose how I spend my working hours and the paths I have followed along the way. My career as an educator has been an expression of who I am as a person and what I value. To me, the two are inextricably linked—my work and me. Without one, the other just would not be the same.

Listen to Your Parents

All children think they know more than their parents do. This is just a fact of life. I thought this way; you probably did too. My children certainly, at some points, saw their mother and me as old fogies, set in our ways and completely out of touch with modern life, with the needs and wants of the younger generation to which they belonged.

This is just the nature of youth. When we are children and young adults, before we have had much real-life experience and seen how the world works, we tend to be self-centered. And in that egotism we believe we know what is best for us, from what time we should go to bed to what to study in school. In one light we can view this as arrogance, as an overinflated sense of our own worth. We are so smart, so insightful, we believe, that we can choose the paths of our lives independently with no input from others. Particularly not from our parents, who surely were never young and could not fathom what it's like to face such overwhelming choices and opportunities.

Though my siblings and I all respected our parents and for the most part got along with them just fine, we each had this streak of rebelliousness in us, this desire to do as we pleased, to have control over our little worlds. And toward that end, to my parents' credit, they gave us a modicum of leeway. They taught us how to make good decisions for ourselves—a necessity when they were working out of state for the majority of the year. Left to our own devices as we were, we could have gotten into an enormous amount of trouble, and I won't lie—sometimes we did. That's another part of being a kid. You're going to mess up no matter how hard you try to stay on the straight and narrow.

Every parent has a golden rule—the one thing (or two or three things) they absolutely require their children to obey. For some this means doing homework right after school instead of leaving it until near bedtime. For others it means no elbows on the dinner table, or no crossing the street alone, or no talking back lest you want to spend the rest of the day in your room.

My parents had rules like that. Such boundaries are necessary for a child because, no matter how confident he feels, he does not know where his limits are. As kids we think we do, but our worlds are small, and we are not able to see the bigger picture. We can't tell how our choices now will affect our lives months or even years down the line. Our parents can, however. They have experience on their side. And that is why it's vitally important to listen to them and follow their directions even when you do not agree.

My parents had a few golden rules by which we lived. We did have to do our homework first thing when we got home from school—a practice I continued with my own children, much to their dismay at times. I felt the same as a child, particularly in the autumn and spring, when the weather was warm and all my friends were allowed to go out and play. I would hear them through my bedroom window as I sat there with my math book open, poring over a problem I had no idea how to solve. But I would have to stay there until I managed to figure it out.

Did I believe this was fair? Of course not. A child doesn't like being different from his peers. He wants to have what they have and do what they do. If they were outside tossing a football around, and I was in my room doing homework, how do you think that made me feel? Like an outcast. Like my parents were the worst in the world. But their word was law in our home, and so I had to do as they said.

Many years later, of course, I realized how wise my parents were to put me on this strict schedule. By requiring that I do my homework before I could go out and play, they instilled in me a great sense of responsibility and a discipline that has stayed with me until this day. Don't get me wrong—I know how important it is to play no matter what your age. We all need that release to keep ourselves balanced and sane. However, I also understand there are certain things in life that are simply necessary to do. There's schoolwork when you're young and chores around the house. When you're older there are bills to pay and work deadlines to meet, among many other things. Our responsibilities grow exponentially as we age, but one thing always remains the same: how we approach them. If we learn early on in life that work must always come before play, we will find success.

As my siblings and I aged, our parents' rules changed right along with us. This was partly because, over time, we mastered what they had taught us to do. By high school none of us complained about homework or housework; those were simply parts of our routine. So Mom and Dad had to think up something new.

The opportunity arose as we began to get our drivers' licenses. We were fortunate in that our parents provided cars for us to use—nothing fancy, just some old, used clunkers to take us to school and our friends' houses and home again. But that was all we were allowed to do. There would be no joy-riding, no cruising around town just to show off our wheels. And most important, we would not have more than one friend in the car with us at a time.

Seems like a funny rule, doesn't it? What's the use of having a car if you can't play chauffeur for all your friends? This was especially true for me as I was the only one in my social circle who could drive. Still, my father remained firm: I was not to have a bunch of boys in my car, period. There would be no discussion on the matter.

At first, of course, I thought this, too, was unfair. I got top grades; I worked part time; I contributed to the household. I did everything my parents told me. So why couldn't I take the gang out for a spin once in a while? I didn't hang around with hoodlums; all my friends were good kids just like me.

However, that didn't matter to Dad. Having been a boy himself once, and seeing what went on around our neighborhood, he knew how dangerous a group of young males could be. One friend in the car was fine. That would not distract me from my driving. But two or three, or five or six? That was a recipe for disaster. The group mentality would take over, and my thoughts would no longer be my own. Before I knew it I would be racing up the road or driving off somewhere he had explicitly told me not to go.

"This vehicle is for *you*, Willie," Dad told me while going over these basic rules. "It's not for your friends. If they want to get in trouble, let them do it in someone else's car."

And of course I did what my father said. I didn't like it, but I obeyed because by then I knew that was my duty as his son. I also listened because if he caught me driving a group of friends around, he said, he would take away my keys, and who knew if I would ever get them back? I valued the freedom my car gave me too much to risk losing it.

Again, when I had children of my own, and they began to come of age, I instituted this rule as well, especially for my sons. I gave them both cars when they earned their licenses, but they came with a caveat: no more than one friend at a time. The rule was met with the same resistance I had given my dad way back when. But my boys never did get in any serious trouble, so I suppose it worked, just as it had for me.

My father's second golden rule was: never take anything that doesn't belong to you. When you're young it's easy to covet your friends' possessions. Maybe one has a bike, and you don't. Another has a nice pair of sneakers you know would just look so good on your feet. It would be easy to take these things or to bully these friends into giving them to you. But that's the easy way out, and as we've seen, that was never an option as far as my father was concerned. If I wanted something, I had to earn it. I had to work for it. Maybe that meant mowing lawns around town to scrape up a few dollars or saving my weekly allowance until I had enough to purchase the object of my dreams.

Again, I saw this all as a hassle when I was young. What kid doesn't operate solely on instant gratification? I saw something I wanted, and I had to have it right away. I couldn't wait, and just taking it would be so much easier. But for fear of disappointing my dad or making him angry, I complied with his advice. Sometimes the wait was interminable while I worked to raise the funds for whatever it was I desired, but when I finally got it, the reward was sweet. I valued those things that I earned for myself so much more than anything that had been handed to me.

In raising my children, I've followed my parents' examples in so many ways. And now that they are all adults, it's easy to see that the payoff has been abundant. My sons and daughter are happy, successful, and intelligent individuals who understand their own worth and the value of making their own ways in the world. Not that my wife and I haven't helped them; of course we are always here for them no matter what sort of assistance they need. But as they've grown older, their requests have grown fewer and further between, and their independence has truly flourished. I know this is because I taught them discipline and responsibility from the very start, as my parents did with me.

I did enact one rule, however, that deviated from my parents' course. When my children were in school, each of them had to learn to play a musical instrument. Which one they chose was up to them. My mandate was simply that they attended the lessons and practiced every day.

What was the point of this? It wasn't that I loved music so much or that I longed to hear trumpets blaring and drums banging throughout the house. The fact is that being able to read and play music is a key to success in academics. It teaches patience and discipline and critical thinking, not to mention creativity. It exercises all parts of the brain and makes it easier then to excel in other subjects. If you can read a sheet of music, you can solve a math problem. It's as simple as that.

So what did they choose? Our oldest child, Wyvondalynn, played the clarinet and piano. She has also always been an amazing singer; with her voice, she could win *American Idol* in a minute. She studied in all three areas throughout high school but did not continue it into college, and that was fine with my wife and me. Our requirement was for high school only. What our children chose to pursue in college was up to them. Regardless, she graduated second in her class at Elizabeth City

State University and went on to get an MBA from High Point College, both in North Carolina. I like to think her earlier musical training had something to do with her success.

Our second child, Steven, played the trumpet. In high school he joined the band and did well, but there was one hitch: he was also the quarterback on the school's football team, which meant he could not do the marching band half-time shows as he was playing in the games. My wife and I granted him a waiver on this as he was at least participating in something else. He did not continue to pursue music in college either, but he graduated from Elizabeth City State University, went on to the Brody School of Medicine of East Carolina University on a full scholarship, and is now practicing medicine in Charlotte, North Carolina. Sounds like another success story to me.

Our youngest, Willie II, really took to our music requirement. It seemed he played every instrument he could in high school—saxophone, percussion, keyboards, sousaphone, you name it, he tried it. Unlike his siblings he did join the band at his Elizabeth City State University, but after a while he stopped so he could focus on his studies. He graduated with a degree in computer science and then went to North Carolina A&T State University, where he earned a master's in computer software engineering as well.

Willie also took another different route from our other two children: at one point he said he wanted to drop out of college. He felt my wife and I were spending too much money on him, and he figured he could join the army or something like that and make his own way. But as far as I was concerned, no such thing would happen because dropping out of university was not his decision to make. Sure, I could have told him to follow his heart and do what he wanted, to go out into the world and find himself if that was what he really wanted to do. But where would that have gotten him? Wandering as a way of life might be good for some people, but that was not how my children were going to live their lives. My wife and I had put a lot of time and effort (not to mention money) into raising them to be responsible, intelligent, motivated individuals, and while of course we wanted Willie to do what made him happy, we were not going to let all those years of hard work—his and ours—go to waste.

This is a great departure from how parents deal with their children these days. As an educator I have seen the trends change over the years. It used to be children listened to what their parents said and obeyed their orders. These days, it seems, it's the other way around. A child (and by that I mean a son or daughter of any age, from preschooler to college student) will tell his mom and dad, "I want this," or "This is what I want to do," and the parents will bend over backward to get it for him or to make his desires happen. Thus our younger generations have become demanding and impatient; they expect to get what they want exactly when they want it without having to do much work to get it.

Obviously this was not how I raised my children. Using my parents' example from when I was coming up, I made sure my sons and daughter knew there is a price to pay for anything they truly want, and they will pay it with their determination and exertion. Meaning what they put into it is what they will reap in the end. There are no shortcuts in life, not if you want to be able to look yourself in the eye each morning in the bathroom mirror and be proud of you who are and what you have accomplished or what you are still striving to achieve. I have known that feeling of pride, and I hope my children have as well and will continue to experience it over and over throughout their lives.

And that's why Jacqueline and I told Willie he could not drop out of college. We appreciated his looking out for our finances, but that was not a concern for us. We'd known for a long time we'd have three children to put through college, and we'd made our arrangements. Perhaps he was just feeling stressed out at the time due to schoolwork or some other issue; perhaps he had a bit of wanderlust. What young person doesn't? Whatever the case, his mother and I sat him down and told him what we expected of him: until he had his diploma in hand, he was still to abide by our rules. Our main concern was that he and our other two children earn their degrees so that whatever roads they took in life, they would always have that accomplishment to bolster them.

⁓

While I tried to emulate my parents in raising my children, times have changed, so parenting styles have had to change too. These days we face issues and problems of which my parents never would have dreamed: epidemic substance abuse, children being medicated for ADD and depression, so much technology it's difficult at times to get a kid to go out into the sunshine and run around for a while.

In my household, though, I stuck to the old traditions as much as our modern times would allow. My rules for my children were fairly basic. First, no tattoos. That one was nonnegotiable. While a bright-orange tiger etched into your forearm might seem like a great idea when you're eighteen, it will probably be nothing but a hindrance and an embarrassment just five years later, when you're looking for work in the professional field you've chosen.

Second, my children were not to come home with any crazy haircuts. While these would not be permanent like tattoos, I did not want them walking around town looking like clowns. I wanted them to be known for their brains and personalities, not for some silly temporary eccentricity.

These are just a couple of examples. It's fair to say my wife and I ruled our house with a bit of an iron fist; we had many regulations, large and small, and we expected our children to know them and follow them. Just as I had sat in my room as a child, struggling over math problems while listening to my friends playing outside, I required my sons and daughter to complete their homework in their rooms—to avoid distractions—until dinnertime. After we ate together as a family, I would go outside with the boys and throw a football around or play basketball or even just sit on the back patio and talk. And Jacqueline spent plenty of quality time with our daughter as well. When we were through with those activities, if there was time left before bedtime, the kids could watch TV or play videogames. This was our routine, and we did not deviate from it.

And of course they did not like any of it very much. I heard more than my fair share of complaints and moans, especially in the spring and autumn months, when none of them liked to be stuck indoors during daylight hours, holed up with their schoolbooks. But as they aged and became more cognizant of the reasons behind my rules, they understood. They got that it was for their own good and that as their parent, it was my job to guide them toward whatever was in their best interests. They still gave me flak at times, of course, but the argumentative episodes were fewer and further between.

When they got older, the rules had to change—or, rather, Jacqueline and I had to add to them. As our children reached dating age, we had to set some ground rules to help them navigate that new and often confusing landscape. Our first and foremost rule was that none of them could date more than one person at a time, especially the boys. I just didn't see the purpose of running around with this person and that one and this one too. That would lead only to confusion and heartbreak, and it would send my sons and daughter an erroneous message: that it was okay for them to do whatever they wanted to do, even when it concerned the feelings of other people. I am proud to say that they always respected this rule and never questioned it. When they stopped seeing someone and took up with someone new, they let me know. Aside from teaching them accountability, it was an excellent means of keeping our lines of communication open. It let them know that they could talk to my wife and me about anything, no matter how personal.

Now I don't want to be misleading here: we did give the kids perks for following the house rules. A little reward now and then always boosts our motivation to do things we don't necessarily like. One of the biggest perks we offered was new cars for all our children as they entered their senior years in high school. As long as they worked hard up until that point, as long as they got consistently good grades and did all they could to obtain scholarships and grants for their upcoming college enrollments, Jacqueline and I felt they deserved such prizes. Granted, these were not lavish, brand-new, high-end automobiles. No, they were used and within a particular price range but in good shape and mechanically sound. Still, you'd think we had bought them each the newest-model BMW. They drove those wheels around town with an enormous amount of pride because they knew that they had earned them.

As my children became adults and began having children of their own, I was very curious to see how they would handle discipline and rules in their own homes. Would they follow my and my father's leads, instituting golden rules and teaching their kids about responsibility and hard work from an early age? Or would they go the route of so many young parents today and ask "how high?" whenever their children tell them to jump?

Of course I hoped for the former. And I have been delighted—not to mention a bit vindicated—to see that both my sons and my daughter run their households just as I ran mine: with rules and rewards, with accountability and a good work ethic. Seems they did decide to listen to their parents after all.

———

Being a parent is a lifelong job. Come to think of it, so is being a parent's child. Neither of these roles diminishes as both parties age; you will always be your mother and father's son or daughter whether you're an infant, a teenager, or a senior citizen, and they will always be Mom and Dad to you.

My mother was one who seemed to know this well. Even when she and Dad were hundreds of miles away for months at a time, she did all she could to keep our family together. She called us on the phone every day when she got home from work; she checked up on us so much that my siblings and I always felt like Mom was watching even when she wasn't there.

However, we weren't the only objects of her attention. Prior to marrying Dad and having children, she had come from a large family, with parents and siblings but also more aunts, uncles, and cousins than she could count after a while. And even when she had her own family to look after, she always made the time to stay in touch with the Lusters, her family of origin. She always knew the latest goings on in even the most remote branches.

Mom kept this up well into the later years of her life through regular letters and phone calls. (This was back in the 1950s and '60s, long before e-mail and text messaging were even thoughts in someone's mind.) Unfortunately she didn't get to see some of her relatives as much as she would have liked. They lived too far away, and who has the time—not to mention the money—to travel that much when they're working full time and raising kids? But she thought about them every day, and at some point in that rumination an idea struck her: why not have a reunion? A gathering, a big party that everyone could attend. That way they could all see each other at once and catch up without having to make multiple trips around the country or choose who to visit based on financial constraints.

When she ran the idea past her family members, every one of them agreed it was brilliant.

So Mom set to work. She would host the first-ever Luster family reunion in Madison, Florida, the following year as it would take that long to plan. There were so many factors to consider. What kinds of foods should she serve, and where should she get them from? Or should she cook them all herself? No, better to order from local restaurants maybe; the preliminary head count for the reunion had already reached triple digits, and the invitations hadn't even gone out yet. Then there had to be decorations and activities, and she would have to contact some hotels in the area to see if they would offer any discounts or reserve blocks of rooms.

She had help in all these tasks, of course. Dad pitched in where he could. It was wonderful in a way to bring this thing to life, to put their heads together and come up with what would be a truly memorable three-day weekend—that was how long most visitors were planning to stay. By the time the beginning of summer rolled around, we were ready. All we had to do was wait for the guests to arrive.

And arrive they did. In the couple of days prior to the date when the reunion would start, Dad made so many trips to the airport to pick people up, he must have filled the car's gas tank a dozen times. Some incoming relatives took taxis straight to the hotels they had chosen as their home bases, and others rented cars. It seemed no one could wait to get the party started. In all, about 150 people showed up for the event, which was held at a park on a beautiful summer afternoon. We had a stroke of luck with the weather—the sky was blue, and the sun kept us warm, but it wasn't too hot. The sounds of joyous laughter and animated conversations filled the air as we got our fill of the great food and drink Mom had provided—and of each other. Still, when it was over, no one wanted to go home. So they promised one another they would do it again. In fact they'd hold a reunion every two years with a different family hosting each time.

And so a tradition was born. For almost fifteen years—even after my mother's untimely death in 1977—the reunions continued in Florida, New York, New Jersey, and other places. Every two years, like clockwork, every relative who could made his or her way to the chosen destination for three days of fun and family love. The hosts always tried to come up with interesting things to do in their neck of the woods; there were side trips to amusement parks and baseball games and trips on fishing boats. Those folks who couldn't or didn't care to get around that much simply met up in smaller groups to spend some quality time together. And then, of course, there was always the reunion itself, the big party that all would attend. Every one of them was just as fun as that first one back in Madison, Florida, had been.

Sometime in the 1990s the reunions stopped. I can't say exactly why; I imagine life just got in the way, and one or two postponements led to the fadeout of the entire tradition. People still talked about them, but it was always in a "well, someday…" way. Unfortunately it took twenty years for that someday to come around. The first family reunion in almost two decades just took place in July 2014, and Jacqueline and I were among those in attendance. It was wonderful to see my mother's side of the family again after so long and to meet its newest members, some of whom are young adults by now. There was a good turnout—about 150 guests, just as at the first one that my mom had hosted—and a whole lot of interest in starting up the reunions again. In fact Jacqueline and I, along with my youngest sister, Willie Mae, will be hosting the next Luster family reunion in North Carolina in the summer of 2016.

I feel very good about this turn of events. It will be an honor to have so many generations of my mother's family—my family—in the place I have called home for most of my adult life. Most of all, it's just good to be back in touch again. Like my mother always told me, you should *never* lose the connections you have to those who hold you up, to the family who were and will be there for you no matter how high you rise or how low you fall. We might not live in the same city or even the same state, but I know that if I were in need, I could call any one of the people I just saw at the reunion, and they would do what they could for me. Needless to say, I would do the same for them. I will always have time for family, no matter how busy my day-to-day life might be, because that was how my parents raised me.

Have a Support System

People need people. It's as simple as that. If you are alive and breathing, at some point in your life you will need another human being, whether it's for companionship, to gain information, to assist you in meeting a goal, or any other purpose under the sun. This is the nature of our species. Though there are some true loners among us, they are few and far between. Most of us, on a day-to-day basis, thrive on having each other around.

Now the question is: who are the people you want and need to have in your life? In other words, who is included in your support system? Think about those who have come and gone (and stayed, if you're fortunate) throughout your life—the ones who have helped you become all you are meant to be or at least given you a hand toward reaching that goal in some way. This support can be emotional, spiritual, financial, even physical, whatever you might need at any particular time.

Some people believe that certain individuals come into our lives for specific purposes at just the right time, and our support systems bear this out. Think about the friends you've had in the past who perhaps are not around anymore for one reason or another. How did they enrich your life while they were in it? Maybe they taught you something about yourself or the world or offered you a shoulder to cry on during a difficult time. Or their support could have come in a more concrete form, such as assisting you in applying for college or helping you study for a big test. Whatever it was, do you think it's possible that each one of them was put in your path just for that purpose they fulfilled? And then once their job was done, you drifted apart or one of you moved far away. Somehow you lost touch. But you can look back on that relationship with fondness and gratitude, and I'll bet that other person is thankful for whatever you taught him or her too.

Now your family can be—and in fact should be—a part of your support system as well. But family is different from friends in that they are always there, or at least they should be. I understand that not everyone has ideal relationships with their parents and siblings and other kin. I wish it were otherwise, and it saddens me to think of those who cannot turn to their families in times of need or times of happiness. Those of us who can should consider ourselves fortunate. Having a close, supportive family you can rely on as a safety net is truly a blessing. I am thankful every day that I have experienced that both as a child and as a parent.

And as a husband, don't let me forget that. Because when I grew up, my family support system expanded to include not just my parents, grandparents, aunts, uncles, and brothers and sisters but my wife and her family as well. When I married Jacqueline, I inherited a whole other set of these same relatives, just with "-in-law" after their names. To me that title didn't mean anything. They always have been and always will be my family because they are always there for me.

I met Jacqueline during my first semester at Elizabeth City State University in North Carolina. I was having a bit of a hard time then, it being my first time away from my family support system, which I'll get into more later; here I'll just say that meeting and getting to know her was one of the factors that helped me continue on what was, at the time, a difficult journey for me. We were in a class together; I don't remember now which one. I thought she was pretty, and I knew she was smart, so I managed to get her to talk to me. Then we started studying together. And the rest, as they say, is history. We dated for three years then we got married while we were still in school. And now, forty-two years later, we're still going strong.

But it hasn't always been quite that easy. See, just as I was coming into the relationship with my own support system, so was Jacqueline. Her parents and siblings might not have been right there with her every day, but they were still looking out for her. Particularly her dad. When she shared with him the joyous news, during their weekly phone call, that she'd found a boyfriend on campus, his first reaction was distrust—like any good father's would be, especially about a young man he isn't able to see in person. Then Jacqueline mentioned I was from New York, and that really sealed the deal.

"I won't tell you what to do," her dad told her, "because you are a grown woman, and you have a level head, and you can make your own decisions. But, Jacqueline, I will tell you this: New Yorkers are trouble. They are nothing but city slickers who think they can get one over on the rest of us. You just watch out for this fella. If he talks bad to you or starts to seem sort of shady—run the other way!"

This review did not bolster my confidence much. It turned out her father also thought Jacqueline was only dating me because her twin sister already had a boyfriend, and she was feeling left out. Like I was just some flash in the pan, a boy to keep her busy and take her out on Friday nights. But that is not at all what it was. The more I talked to Jacqueline, the more time I spent with her, and the more I got to know her as a person, the more enthralled I was with her because she was—and is—just an amazing person. And I guess she thought I was okay, too, because regardless of what her dad thought about me and her reasons for being with me, we persisted. And I could not have had a more perfect partner by my side all these years. She is the main post that holds up my safety net.

In time, thankfully, I got to meet Jacqueline's family, and once they started to learn some about me, they saw I wasn't all bad. In fact I wasn't bad at all. Soon enough they fully endorsed our dating and later our engagement and our marriage. And in all the time Jacqueline and I have been together, I feel as though I have been together with all of her family as well. They have been there for us in so many ways, both physically and spiritually—offering a literal hand when we needed one or counsel in times of stress or large decisions. My wife and I always have made it a point to support ourselves financially, so we've never had to depend on her parents (or anyone else, for that matter) in this area. But when it comes to good advice and just being around, they have offered us so much more than I ever had expected when Jacqueline made that first call home.

In the true spirit of give and take, my wife and I always include ourselves in the support systems of our close friends and families. We recognize and acknowledge that, as they say, no man is an island, and just as we need assistance sometimes, so do those around us. Some need a lot, some a little; some will come right out and ask, while others will keep it bottled up until their need becomes so great, they're no longer able to hide it, and their world comes crumbling down. Those are the cases where support is most important. When someone you love is on their knees, it is crucial that you bend down and help to lift them up.

It would be great if we could all be more straightforward with one another about the ways in which we need support. But it's difficult for many of us to be that open. I attribute that to a myriad of factors, including how we are raised by our families and the experiences we've had along the way that have taught us to keep our hands away from the fire lest we get burned. Once you are hurt badly enough, you tend to keep any vulnerabilities to yourself so as not to expose yourself to any further pain. That's a human reaction, a form of self-preservation, and unfortunately, in the world today, it's almost a necessary attitude to have at times.

But I'm here to tell you it doesn't always have to be like that. Maybe you feel like you have no support system right now. And maybe you truly don't. But that doesn't mean it's the end and no one will ever help you again in your life. As I mentioned earlier, people come into and go out of our lives multiple times over; in some phases we are friend-rich and others we might as well be living on Antarctica for what little human contact we have. Everything is a cycle in life; everything comes around if you can just hold out long enough to see it happen. If you can't find anyone else in your life who can tell you this, I will do it right here and now: it gets better. Whatever you're going through, in most cases, will pass. If it cannot pass then you'll find a way to deal with it. You are stronger than you know and smarter than you think and absolutely much more capable of great things than you give yourself credit for. These are the ideas a solid support system will reinforce to you.

Since I brought up marriage, let's look into that topic for a minute. Another belief of mine is that parents model what relationships should or should not be for their children. If you and your spouse are always arguing, yelling, even throwing things at one another, what will your young ones learn? That love is volatile, that commitment involves overwhelming emotions, and that when things get too difficult, you can become violent or even give up on the relationship altogether.

On the other hand, if you and your partner act kind to one another, speak only positively in your home, and work calmly, as a team, on creating inclusive solutions to any problems that emerge, your children are going to see the truth: that marriage is a partnership, a little support system unto itself, in which both people must treat each other with respect. Of course it involves emotions; you wouldn't marry someone if you didn't love them, or at least I hope you wouldn't. But there is no room for tempestuousness here. There is never a situation in which it is okay to become physically aggressive against your husband or wife. You're going to hit some rough seas; the trick is working together to keep the rudder steady.

I do, however, understand that marriages do not always work out this well. Sometimes in the beginning it all seems good, but people can change over time in ways we might not have expected. Honestly I never believed in divorce, not for myself at least; I saw it as a relatively easy out that allows people to avoid thinking in advance about the choices they make. But then some people I love dearly found themselves at that crossroads, where they faced the decision of continuing on in unhappy marriages, in relationships that were past the point of salvaging, or face up to it and go their separate ways. Really, the only solution they could come to was the dissolution of their marriages. To stay in them would have been just a punishment for all involved. And that certainly opened my eyes.

These days I see divorce as a very sad and unfortunate but

sometimes necessary thing. I wish it would never happen to anyone, but I understand that in some cases it must. It doesn't mean those involved are bad people or even unhappy people. Quite the contrary, they mostly go on to lead good lives. They have jobs and children and roofs over their heads, and good times are as plentiful for them as for the rest of us.

As major players in the support systems of our sons and daughter, my wife and I have sustained a model of marriage that we hoped would inspire them, particularly when they were young and most impressionable. I have always wanted them to have all they desire in life, including happy and fulfilling relationships. I want them to know love like their mother and I do and like my parents did. My mom and dad remained married until death did they part, just like their vows said; they were together in this life until my mother passed away. I saw them go through thick times and thin, through enough ups and downs to create an entire amusement park full of roller coasters. And through it all they held on to one another, and they kept going. That is the essence of what a marriage is. It is what I have with Jacqueline, and it is, thankfully, what my children have grown up to find with their own spouses.

———

My parents were special people in so many ways. They sacrificed so much for us kids—their whole lives really. They worked; they traveled for work; that was about the extent of it. They had personal interests, of course, but little downtime in which to pursue them. If it was not directly related to supporting my siblings and me financially, spiritually, and emotionally, it just was not a priority for them.

They also gave each other this support. They had to, really. If they did not work together in life, they would not have been able to withstand the long hours of sometimes-backbreaking work they did to earn money. There had to be plans and consensus to keep the operation moving smoothly. Though I did not understand this dynamic at the time because I was a child, in my later years I've come to appreciate the level of commitment my parents had to have with one another in order to make their lives work on a day-to-day basis.

And they kept it rolling like a well-oiled construction rig right up until the late 1970s, when I was preparing to go to college. Wrapped up in my own little world and this new cosmos I was about to thrust myself into, I was not paying particular attention to what was going on with my parents. We were all living in Rochester, New York, by then, so I saw them every day. But we were rather in our own orbits. Their jobs continued to take up much of their time and schoolwork mine, especially as I was going through the process of applying to universities.

However, there was more to it than that. Not long after we had moved to Rochester, some six years or so before this time, my older brother, Johnny, had been killed in a gang-related fight. It had been unexpected and one of the biggest shocks of our lives. Perhaps especially for me, as Johnny was my closest brother in age. We had been pals all along; he had always looked out for me, and I looked up to him. That day he was hanging out with some boys he should not have been with in a place he should not have gone. Knowing he was there, I told my father, who sent me to collect Johnny. But by the time I got there, it was too late. He was gone.

That was on March 27, 1963—a date I will never forget. And on April 16 of that same year, my mother delivered the last of my five siblings, a baby girl. It was a confusing time, with one life ending and a new one coming in, and the rest of us just trying to figure out how we could go on. It was good, I suppose, that Mom had my little sister to tend to. That gave her something to do, so many little tasks on which to focus her attention. But it did not erase what had happened from her mind. She continued to love all of us with all her heart; I never doubted that or stopped feeling it. But she was not the same after Johnny passed. A light had gone out of her; when she wasn't working, she preferred to spend most of her time alone, as if being around people was just too much to bear. Perhaps the laughter of her remaining son reminded her too much of Johnny's. Maybe she just couldn't handle feeling happiness again herself.

Being still a boy, I did not know how to help my mother through this. I wanted to support her. I loved her with all my heart, too, and of course I would have done anything to help. But what could I do? We were all mourning Johnny for a long time. I'm not sure any of us has ever really stopped. But I had lost a brother; she had lost a *son*. Much later, when I became a parent myself, the enormity of that statement, the crushing sadness and mindlessness and unfairness of the event, hit me with a clarity it had not before. If the same were to happen to me, I knew, it would hollow me out just as it had done to my mother.

Unfortunately, instead of getting better, she only got worse. The years went on, and still she kept herself isolated from the world. We all got used to it. Another part of loving someone is meeting them on their own ground, and if this was what she would be capable of for the rest of her life then we would all have to find a way to relate to her in this different environment. Maybe we would never see her big, warm smile again, only the melancholy sort of half-smirk she would grant us once in a while when she caught my siblings and me tussling on the living room floor. Maybe there would be no more raucous dinners where we were all jumping up around the table and pointing at one another, laughing through our mock debates on everything from who would win the World Series to what brand of cereal was the best. This was a different world for all of us now, and that would just have to be okay.

Eventually, somehow, my mom's loneliness took a toll on her health. She began to feel sick more frequently—mysterious stomach pains, headaches that would keep her in bed in the dark all day. Mostly she carried on her life as usual, but she seemed always to be at a doctor's or taking one pill or another, none of which seemed to do a thing.

One night I caught her coming in from work as I sat at the dining room table, going over some paperwork. I had already graduated from college by that time and started my first job, Jacqueline and I were living with my parents for six months to save some money. I had students' test papers spread out across the table and a pen in my hand. It must have been eight o'clock at night.

"Hey, baby," Mom said as she slipped silently into the dining room. Her voice was so gentle, soft like velvet, as comforting as a warm blanket. She came over and put her hand on my shoulder. "What are you up to?"

"Just grading tests," I told her, and she nodded, keeping her eyes on the table. She looked a bit run down. There were dark circles under her eyes, and she was sniffling. She pulled a Kleenex from the pocket of her work uniform and dabbed at her nose then stuffed the tissue back in again.

"Mom, are you feeling all right?" I asked. "Maybe you should take a couple days off work."

She waved her hand at me, dismissing the thought. "Oh, no," she replied in typical Mom fashion, speaking lightly so as not to make me worry. "I got a swine flu shot a couple days ago, and I'm just having a little reaction. It's totally normal. They even tell you at the doctor's office that it might happen. Give me another day, and I'll be right as rain again."

And, of course, she was Mom, so I believed her. She kissed me on the cheek and went up to bed. I turned back to what I'd been doing, my mind completely immersed.

This was in the end of September, and by Halloween, my mother was still sick. She was going to work as usual; she would literally have to lose a limb to take a day off, and even then, if she could get it bandaged up good, she might take just half a day. So while her lingering flu symptoms concerned me, I did not see them as very serious. None of us did. Just a bug, we thought. An early fall cold. Something that would pass in time, maybe when the weather started to change. No one was giving up on her, least of all my father. But I felt it was my duty as her son to keep her going, to talk her through this new bout of illness. I guess it was reassurance for myself, too. I didn't want to admit it, but I was worried about her.

When Christmas came she looked worse than ever. She was coughing a lot more and always pulling her sweater closed around her to fight off what seemed like constant chills. She had been sleeping a lot, and that afternoon Dad had heard her vomiting in the bathroom, though she hadn't mentioned it to him. He wanted her to check in to the hospital to get some tests done, as the prescriptions her doctor had been giving her might as well have been sugar pills for all the good they did. But she refused every time he brought it up. Maybe after the holidays, she said, she would think about it.

A week into the new year, Dad finally got his wish but not in the way he had hoped. Mom had woken up barely able to breathe, practically choking every time she coughed.

"That's enough now," he told her and then bundled her up and put her in the car. He drove right to the hospital; she was admitted quickly and diagnosed with pneumonia at quite an advanced state. Dad called my siblings and some of Mom's family to come. There was barely time to get there before Mom passed. It was January 1977, and she was fifty-three years old.

It's been more than thirty years, and it's still difficult for me to tell that story. My mom's life had a tragic end, one none of us had expected for her. After Johnny died she pulled away from her support system, from us, at a time when she probably needed it most. Am I saying that if she had let us help her more, she would still be with us today? Not at all. That would be like laying blame, and that is one thing I will never do. Each of us reacts to trauma and grief in our own way, and hers was to box it up and put it on the highest shelf in her closet, the one she couldn't even reach without a ladder. She had to keep what she felt to herself and turn off her emotions so she could keep soldiering on. It wasn't that she didn't need us anymore or that she abandoned us. We were all still there, doing what we could to hold that net up high for her, to meet her where she was. I like to think we did all we could given the circumstances; at least that is what I hope—that after so many years of being there for us, in the end we gave her what she needed in a way she could accept. Most of all I just hope that she knew how much she was appreciated and respected and loved.

With Mom gone, of course Dad had a difficult time. He'd lost a son then his wife, and his children were growing and moving away, making the family nucleus smaller and smaller. My little sister was still at home, just in the middle of seventh grade, so he still had her. And eventually he did remarry—not because he didn't love Mom but because he needed a companion in his life, a sentiment I'm sure many of us can understand. He stayed in good health through his later years and never stopped getting around on his own, which was important to him. Many elderly folks consider losing mobility—whether it's not being able to drive due to failing eyesight or legs that don't work as good as they used to—tantamount to the end. Dad is fortunate that he sustained his vigor.

However, that doesn't mean he didn't have accidents. Once, in 2009, my stepmother called and told me that he'd fallen and couldn't get up. She had called for an ambulance, and the EMTs got him righted and took him to the hospital. He'd hit his head—a serious bump. He didn't last for two weeks, but my siblings and I were all there for him the whole time. He was eighty-eight when he passed away.

After Dad's death, just through a routine conversation with my stepmother, I learned that when he had checked in to the hospital, a physical exam had showed there were several bruises on his head—under his hair, where they were not clearly visible. This indicated he had fallen before and, apparently, not told anyone. My stepmother knew he was unsteady and had seen him tumble once or twice, but he had recovered just fine. She hadn't told my siblings and me just because she didn't want to worry us.

As for the other falls…I can only imagine it was that mobility issue. My father was always a strong man, physically and mentally, and I'm sure the vagaries of old age did not sit very well with him. He probably did not like being slow and unsteady in body or in mind, and—like his current wife—did not think there was anything to be alarmed about. I wish he had told me. I don't know what I would have done, but as a member of his support system, I would have rallied the troops and figured something out. My consolation is that while he kept this secret, he was living his life exactly as he wanted. He was happy, and he was proud of the children he had molded and raised. In the end, perhaps one couldn't wish for more than that.

—

At every point in your life—no matter whether your parents are married or divorced, blissful or combative; whether your relationship or your life or career is going exactly as you'd planned or not—you will have friends. Again, as I keep saying, or so I hope. Because friends play very important roles in the development of our characters and even our outlooks on life. They give us that outsider's perspective and present us with worldviews that have *not* been tinted (or tainted) by our family structures. They listen to our hopes and dreams noncritically, in ways that our parents can't because they have too big a stake in them. They laugh with us at silly jokes and cry at sad movies and tell us he or she was a jerk anyway when a paramour dumps us. They give us business advice. They become our partners. Our confidants. Our equals and our complements and, most important, an integral part of our support systems.

I cannot count the friends I've had over the years of my life. All the kids in the neighborhood when I was young and a whole other set of them at school. College study buddies and roommates, career mentors, and the neighbors who lived next door when Jacqueline and I bought our first house. A friendship can happen anywhere, even with the person you'd least suspect. You might not seem to have anything in common on the surface, but if you talk a little while, you see just how closely your interests align. And then you'll talk and talk some more and always be discovering new things about each other, because friendships can run very deep. It can take a lifetime and then some to truly get to know another person.

I have been fortunate in that I've also found friends right within my own family—a kind of two-for-one as far as my support system is concerned. Both were my brothers-in-law. James was my confidant; I could talk to him about the most profound thoughts and topics and trust that he would never tell a soul. Willie, my other brother-in-law, was also my neighbor for twenty years. We kept a garden together; we owned property jointly. We helped one another in our business endeavors, and he even followed my lead, becoming a principal of an elementary school at one point. As we lived next door to one another, our children, of course, were the best of friends also and were constantly invading both of our homes. But Willie and I had an agreement: he gave me authority over his kids, and I let him discipline mine as he saw fit too. We just had that level of trust (and, thankfully, good children who didn't get into too much trouble). You don't see that kind of teamwork in too many extended families today.

Willie and I especially had a lot of give and take in our relationship, and this, you could say, is the essence of a support system: I help you, you help me, and obviously we both benefit. No matter who the person in your system is, he or she must tacitly agree to engage in this dynamic. Friends or family, it works the same. Of course, we don't enter into such a relationship with this in mind; we're not supposed to think, *Well, I can do this for him today, so then he'll owe me, and he'll have to do whatever I want tomorrow.* That's not a support system; that's just shady and really benefits no one.

What I mean by give and take is this: I married Jacqueline when I was twenty-two years old. In the same year I graduated from college. Needless to say we were pretty broke and would continue to be until we got our careers underway. What with paying for bills and housing, we'd really be scraping by with little chance of saving money or investing in our future.

That was where my parents, the charter members of my support system, stepped in to help. Without our asking them for assistance or even hinting that we might need some, they proposed an idea to Jacqueline and me: we could live with them for six months, rent and bill free, so we could work and save up all our money. We wouldn't have to pay for a thing, not even the food we would eat. The offer astounded us; no, it floored us. We were newlyweds, just starting out in the world, and honestly a bit daunted by all the adult responsibilities we were about to take onto our shoulders. We knew we would succeed eventually as long as we supported each other and worked hard toward our common goals.

But this gift that my parents gave us…well, it just made things a whole lot easier for us. Or at least a good deal less stressful. We said yes, of course, and moved in with my mom and dad, which was kind of nice. I'd been away for four years by then, except for summers and the short breaks between semesters. After my rocky start at the university, I'd managed to find my way and become a pretty independent, self-sustaining individual. I'd worked hard at it, and I was proud of myself.

However, there's just something about being back in your childhood home. It was a comfort; it was a joy. During those six months Jacqueline and I stayed with my parents, we were happy and peaceful. We had room to breathe and time to think, allowing us to make our plans without the stress of looming deadlines. And when our time there was up, we had saved enough for the down payment on our first home together. Four years later, when Jacqueline and I decided to move from New York to North Carolina, her parents took us in for another six months, and we saved up enough to have a brand-new house built for us.

In giving of themselves and opening their homes to us when they were not compelled to do so by any means, our parents helped us to better our situation in life—twice. They were selfless, as all good parents are, and as a direct result my wife and I were afforded the opportunity to find ourselves. This is the true purpose of a support system and the method by which we all should give our support to one another.

If Someone Else Can Do It, So Can You

In 1965 I entered the eighth grade at Edison Technical Industrial High in Rochester, New York—a public school, but all the students were boys, grades eight through twelve. This sort of homogeneity, someone had assumed, might help us focus on our studies and less on chasing girls, and to an extent they had been right. Single-sex schools have been a topic of debate since the dawn of education. Sometimes they work; sometimes they don't. In this case, when I was a kid, it surely did.

Meaning I got good grades. I was a pretty studious young man; remember, my brother Johnny called me a bookworm when I was only thirteen. And that carried on through my teenage years. I played sports too—in fact I was a star athlete at Edison Tech. I was on the football team, but my true love was basketball. I became a starter on the varsity team my sophomore year and stayed there until I was a senior. I knew I was good, and so of course I had dreams of going pro, as all young athletes do at some point. But I was also honest, and I knew I really wasn't *that* good. Big fish in a little pond, as they say. In the sea of the NBA, I probably would have flopped as soon as the first wave struck.

So I focused on my studies as well, knowing that book learning was what would get me ahead in life. I soaked up knowledge and found out all I could about pretty much everything. I'd always had a hunger to know, to find out what was going on in other parts of the world I couldn't experience for myself.

So it only makes sense that I eventually became a teacher, right? Except that back then I had no idea that was what I would do with my life. I didn't have a lot of direction. According to my parents, I would be going to college when the time came but to study what? I had no idea. Medicine seemed interesting. So did law. But so did being an astronaut and orbiting the moon, and so did driving around the country in a convertible car with the top down, a copy of *On the Road* my only passenger.

The problem, as I saw it, was not a dearth of opportunities but an overabundance. There was so much out there to do. How on earth would I ever find the one thing that interested me? This question confounded me for a while. Then it occurred to me: I just had to look around at what the people in my life were doing. Maybe one of them had a job that might appeal to me.

I started, of course, with my parents. But as they had told me time and time again, I was not to follow in their footsteps. So, on to the next. I spent the majority of my time at school, so that seemed a natural place to look around. And there were plenty of different careers there: teachers, administrators, athletics coaches, even cleaning staff. There were the people who tended the grounds or directed the school plays or answered the phones in the main office.

I could do any of those, I thought. But there seemed to be something missing from all of it. Teaching might be a good idea, I thought; it would certainly fill the criteria I'd set for myself—to have a job where I could wear a tie and where people would show me respect. But I just did not relate to any of the teachers at my school. Not even the male ones. I liked their classes and appreciated the instruction they gave me, but there was something missing.

Then one day it occurred to me. There were no African-American teachers at my school. There was no one who *looked like me*.

This might not seem like a big deal, especially if you are not a person of color. But to those who have been historically underrepresented in the professional world (and many other aspects of culture and society), it is a big sticking point. It wasn't that I disliked my teachers or held anything against them because they were all Caucasian. That didn't make them any better at their jobs or any worse. But it did make them, at least in my eyes, different. And I needed to see what *I* might look like in such a position.

Thinking back, I realized that most of my teachers to date had been white. This was the 1960s, remember, so that was fairly par for the course. The nation had been officially integrated about a decade earlier, but a lot of that was on paper.

It had not made it to reality yet, at least not down into the crevices like the public school systems. The only exception I came up with was Mr. Lattimore, my seventh-grade science teacher. He was African-American. Unfortunately, that hasn't made me remember what I learned in his class any better.

But I did learn, at least in retrospect, what an important figure he had been in my life. Even though I hadn't known it at the time—and perhaps he hadn't either; for all I know, he was just an average guy showing up for his job every day and not trying to prove any political points—he was my first role model in education. I watched him teach day after day, going down the same curriculum he followed every year: amoebas, cells, DNA, the building blocks of all matter. But there was a subtle subtext underneath all that, a message meant for me and all the other African-American boys in my class: *if I can do it, so can you.* That was the real point of every word that came out of Mr. Lattimore's mouth.

That didn't mean he wanted all of us to go into education. We could be businessmen, entrepreneurs, community leaders, fighter-jet pilots, movie stars—anything we wanted to be. He was living proof that we could be people of color and do all the same things the Caucasians around us did. We might meet more adversity; in fact, given the times, difficulty was probably a given. But we *could* do it. If we remained strong and diligent, if we educated ourselves and took advantage of opportunities instead of letting them slip by us, we, too, could become who we wanted to be. We could be self-made men regardless of the color of our skin.

That was a heavy message for a fourteen-year-old; no wonder I really couldn't process it intellectually at the time. But the seed was nonetheless planted—the inkling that through hard work I could break down any obstacles in my way. Perhaps that was also the moment when being a teacher had begun to appeal to me, again subconsciously. But it wasn't until about four years later that all these ideas came to the surface. And I was so glad they did.

A Lifelong Lesson

You don't stop having role models just because you get older. All throughout our lives we find people to look up to or mold ourselves after in one way or another. There are always our parents and other family; there are our teachers and those involved in our educations. Later there might be on-the-job mentors or supervisors who inspire us to be all that we can be. The point is to never stop looking for these people who will help you achieve your goals no matter what those goals are and no matter where you are in your life.

I had role models all throughout school, right up through my college graduation. And when I entered the workforce thereafter, I immediately sought out someone from whom I could learn. This was at my first teaching job, at James Madison High School in Rochester, New York, and fortunately I didn't have to look too far or too long to find such a mentor. The school at the time had an African-American principal named

Johnny Wilson. Though I had wanted to be a teacher for years, and finally I had achieved that goal, now I looked at Johnny and thought, *Hm. If he can be a principal, why can't I?*

I couldn't think of one reason why I couldn't. And so, though I was only a couple of years into my teaching position, I decided to go back to school to get the credentials I would need to enter school administration. I enrolled part time at Brockport University, near Rochester, and over the course of several years earned a master's of science in administration. Fresh out of school, I was offered an assistant principalship at Eastside School in Jackson, North Carolina; there I cut my teeth, as they say, for a year then moved on to another assistant's position at Gumberry High School in Jackson, North Carolina. Another year there taught me all I needed to know and gave me the hands-on experience I would need to take with me when I advanced. With all this knowledge in my hands, I accepted my first position as a school principal, at Gumberry High in 1979.

I enjoyed every minute of that job. Don't get me wrong; I had loved teaching. I'd liked being in the classroom, helping young people learn and enrich their minds, but I felt that as a principal I could get more done. I could really get in there and make things happen for these kids in a way I couldn't as a teacher because I just hadn't had the means. On this higher level I had more reach and more pull, and I could use both to better Gumberry High and its students.

And I did so. In my time there, I think, I managed the

school well and instituted some good policies. I kept the machine working, so to speak, which is as much as one can ask for sometimes. However, I never stopped looking ahead, not just for the school but for myself. I had achieved my goal of becoming a principal, so now I had to think: *What's next?* I could easily have stayed in the same office for the rest of my career. Some educators do that—once they reach principal-ship, that's as high as they care to go, so they settle in and chug along until retirement. If that works for them, great. But that's not how I was raised. My parents always told me—and showed me through their example—that I should constantly strive to be more. No matter how well I do, I can always do better. So I kept my eyes on the horizon.

And eventually a new inspiration came into my view. Three years after I'd started my principalship, in 1982, Northhampton County hired its first-ever African-American superintendent of schools. His name was Dr. Willis Mcleod, and it was clear from day one that he was there to get things done. He was very friendly and personable, a real pleasure to have a conversation with. But when it was time for business, he switched on a dime. If you were somehow amiss in your duties, he let you know without pulling any punches. He was no-nonsense; he made it clear that we could talk and laugh and go out for lunch together and have a grand old time, but that didn't mean we could let our responsibilities slip. He held each of us account-able for our own work just as he was accountable for his, and if what we did was not up to his standards, he would let us know in no uncertain terms. I liked that about him. I, too, felt that if you take on a job, you are the only one responsible for your success or failure, and there should be no failure.

So of course I wanted to be just like Dr. Mcleod. It helped, too, that he was a very sharp-looking man. I don't think I ever saw even a speck of dust on his well-shined shoes. He wore nice watches and suits that had to be tailor made, they fit him so well. He was well groomed, with close-cropped hair and always clean shaven. To top it all off, he drove the nicest cars. There was nothing about him that wasn't admirable and much I could model my own life and career after. Toward that end I went back to school again; I enrolled in NOVA Southeastern University in Fort Lauderdale, Florida, and came out three years later with a doctorate of education, administration, and supervision. I accepted the post I mentioned earlier, as associate superintendent of schools for Northampton County, North Carolina, and a year or so later moved on to be the superintendent of nearby Halifax County. And I didn't stop there; twelve years later I took on the last assignment of my career in education, as chancellor of my alma mater, Elizabeth City State University in North Carolina.

With each successive level I achieved over the years, I did so because I had a role model to show me what was possible. I had ambitions of my own, of course; it wasn't like I drifted through my life just waiting for someone to come along who might give me some direction. I wanted first to do the best and the most I could in any position I held, but I also wanted to keep my eyes open for opportunities to do more. Often they became clearer and more visible to me when I saw someone doing something that I'd already decided I would like to do. Getting an objective view of a goal can show us what it would be like to occupy that space ourselves. Seeing someone else doing what we want to do helps us to better picture ourselves in that role. This is one of the most important services a role model can provide.

Invest in Yourself and Your Children

We have lots of sayings about money, don't we? It makes the world go 'round; our love of it is the root of all evil. It grows on trees—or doesn't. It's a good servant but a bad master.

And you can't take it with you when you die.

All of these, I believe, are true. Money complicates matters just as often as it fuels our dreams and launches us toward success. Money makes money—that's another saying that can be true as well. When we have more than we need, we can invest the surplus to increase our supply. When we're just scraping by with barely enough to pay our monthly bills, it seems like we'll never have two dollar bills to rub together again.

I've been on both ends of that equation. Obviously, having more money is better. Money cannot buy happiness—another oldie but goodie—but life is definitely a little easier when you don't have to worry about every penny and plan everything around when your next paycheck will come. Having money allows you to look at the long term, to see that there is a future beyond next week or next month, one in which you will have the means to participate. It helps you map out where you want to go.

Now don't get me wrong: this is not to say that you must have money to participate in life or to meet any of your goals. Money *helps*. It does not *make things happen*. That is entirely up to you. And so no matter how much or how little you have, the best thing you can always do is invest in yourself. What you put in is what you get out, as they say, so if you put nothing into your future, what do you think will happen? Nothing good, I can guarantee that. Or, rather, nothing at all. You will stagnate; you will remain where you are, never advancing, never reaching those dreams you once had for yourself. And that, to me, is one of the worst things that can happen. Good or bad, we need events to occur in our lives to propel us forward. Tragedy or trauma forces us to overcome and achieve in spite of it; the satisfaction of an achievement earned similarly pushes us on to do more and be more.

Investing in yourself will give you a solid foundation from which to take this flight. This means putting money into furthering your education, taking a training course, even buying a new suit—doing whatever is necessary to raise your status in the world and help you become the person you're meant to be. If you don't have a lot of extra money or none at all, this can seem like a pipe dream, but let me tell you: it's not. If you want something bad enough, you'll find a way to make it happen, even if that means postponing today's pleasures for a lifetime of success. This might take the form of not upgrading to the newest smartphone on the market when the one you have works just fine and instead putting the money you would have spent into your college fund. It might be driving your old car for a year or two more before buying a new one so you can afford to buy a laptop instead, on which you can do your homework and keep track of your budget.

The point is that we all must make sacrifices for what we want. Sometimes how much you achieve in life is dependent on how much you're willing to give up.

Diplomas and Dollar Signs

Higher education in the United States costs a lot of money. That's just a cold, hard fact. In 2014, as of this writing, the average cost of a college education is more than twenty-two thousand dollars per year for an in-state public school; a moderately priced private college will run you over forty-four thousand dollars per year. So for a full four-year education, you'd be looking at anywhere from eighty-eight thousand dollars to $176,000, and that doesn't include books and materials, personal expenses, any transportation that might be necessary, food…in short, it really adds up. And if you're not wealthy, it can seem unattainable.

But that is the furthest thing from the truth. So many kids today—and their parents—believe that because they aren't wealthy, they can't go to college. I can understand their negativity. I was fortunate to grow up in an era when a college education was still an affordable undertaking, no loans or grants necessary. But it's not like that today. Now most students must have some sort of financial aid just to get them in the doors of higher education.

And that's the good news because there are *so many* avenues through which a young person can get money for education, from scholarships sponsored by community organizations, churches, and other local venues to state and federal loans and grants. As I used to tell my high-school students, if you're motivated, there is always a way to get it done. It might not be the path you envisioned taking, and you might not like the debt you'll have to start paying back upon graduation. Just try to consider that your monthly payments toward your investment in yourself.

When I was a principal, getting kids to college was one of my main ambitions. Not just that, though; I wanted them to be *excited* about it. I wanted them to look at a higher education as a tool they could carry with them for the rest of their lives. Once you have a degree, after all, no one can take it away from you.

The problem was that so many of them thought college was off limits for them because their parents didn't have enough money. As if they had to walk in on their first day with twenty-two thousand dollars in cash and hand it over before they'd be allowed to set foot in a classroom. That's just not how it works, I would tell them, then I'd steer them to the library or a computer, where they could look into what sort of financial aid packages were out there and available to them. Many—I'd even say most—were amazed by what they found. College, it seemed, was really within their grasp after all. Who would've thought?

The next hurdle was convincing their parents of the same. The truth was that many of these students believed they couldn't afford college because that was what their moms and dads told them. Even when I brought them into my office for a conference, sat them down, and explained how feasible it would be for their children to make this investment in themselves, some didn't believe me, or perhaps they didn't *want* to believe. They had probably never gone to college themselves and didn't have anyone in their lives back then to push them in that direction. They had no one to help them find the information they would have needed about scholarships and grants and such, and so they'd gone their whole lives believing that universities were available only to the rich.

I understood this mind-set. Though my parents had always encouraged me to pursue my education as far as I could, they did not know where I should start or what steps I would need to take. Because I was so dedicated to that dream, I took the initiative to research what I needed to know before jumping in, but no one ever helped me with that. It didn't bother me at the time, when I was young, but as I grew older and now had these students to inspire and motivate, I realized how important it was to have an adviser while in this process.

So no matter how naysaying they or their parents would be, I would not give up. I'd still call them in for meetings; I'd give them literature on different schools I thought would be their perfect match. I talked and talked about it until I just couldn't say another word. And most of the time it worked. With just my nudge in the right direction, these kids and their parents jumped right on a good path, one that would lead them, hopefully, toward a prosperous future. More important, they understood how vital it was to make that investment in themselves.

When you have a child, the first thing you know is that it will be a financial investment in the form of buying diapers, formula, food, toys, clothing, and every other necessity that arises in your little one's life. Most of us know this going in; those who don't find it out soon enough. And few of us, if any, will ever complain about the fact. Because we know these are the things we need to do to help our children grow up healthy, strong, and happy, to become the successful adults we hope they eventually will be.

I've said it before, but it always bears repeating: as parents we always want our children to do better than we've done and have better than we've had. And while that certainly pertains to economics and the material things of life, it also means we want them to be spiritually and emotionally fulfilled. Whatever support we felt we did not get as children, we strive to give to ours. Wherever we saw our own parents and other role models falling short, whether through willful neglect or through cir-cumstances that were beyond their control, we fill in those gaps when we have families of our own. This takes diligence and effort; it takes a concerted, combined focus between you and your partner to ensure that your offspring's lives are full and rounded.

Most important, this effort must start from the very beginning. As soon as your children are born, show them love in ways that they will understand. Before they can speak, it's nonverbal cues such as hugging and cuddling. As they grow older and can communicate more, you can express to them in words how important they are not just to you but to the world at large. All children must understand this: that they are special and unique, with gifts only they can possess and use. They are here for very specific purposes, whether that's to cure a disease or raise a family or play beautiful music that brings joy to all those who hear it. No matter what they do, they are valuable. This is the message we must ensure they hear.

We can also invest in our children by helping them achieve their dreams. If they want to go to school, we have to assist them in paying tuition. If they want to start a business, give a little seed money to help them get it off the ground. If you simply don't have the financial resources then give your precious time and attention to your children and bestow it freely. Money will come and go; this they will understand. And there is always a way to find what they need when they need it. As long as you're there to boost them up, they'll have the strength to go after their goals regardless of the cost because children who know they are worthy grow up to be adults who achieve great things.

My wife and I have been blessed with the financial means

to help our three children reach their educational goals, and we're continuing that support with the next generation of the Gilchrist family. All our grandchildren have savings accounts into which I make monthly deposits, starting when they're three months old. By the time they're twenty-one, they've got nest eggs to do with as they please. Of course their parents and I hope they'll use the money to go to college, but in the end the choice will be up to them. Who knows? Twenty-one years from now, higher education might not even exist.

In that case, or if they decide that college just isn't the route they want to take, they can use my investment in them to pay for a wedding, as a down payment on a home or car, or to travel around the world if that's what will make them feel like happy and fulfilled individuals. The end result is not my concern as much as the investment is because in making that commitment to each child every month, I ensure they know that I value them and that I want to give them the best future possible—whatever "best" means to them.

I make this sacrifice because I don't want my grandchildren to start out in life trying to dig out of a financial hole. And if you can manage it, I highly recommend that you do the same for your children or grandkids or whomever you have. You don't have to be wealthy; you don't have to sock away five hundred dollars or more a month. If five dollars is all you can afford, that's better than nothing. It's an investment regardless of the amount.

Over the years, Jacqueline and I have invested not only in our own children but in the sons and daughters of our family and friends. We took in three nephews at three different times, both of whom were having trouble at home and at school. They needed a change of scenery, a break from their bad routines, and my wife and I could provide that for them. We gave them food and a place to sleep, and we treated them just like we did our sons and daughter, with all the expectations we placed on them. It took some time—any great shift in character does—but those boys eventually came around. When they graduated from high school, one went on to be a marine, and the other is a lawyer. We couldn't be prouder of either of them if they were our own children.

Another nephew of ours got into some similar trouble. He and his parents just couldn't see eye to eye, and his high-school principal was ready to throw him out over excessive absences, failed classes, and a general disinterest in learning. This boy was in a bad spot; he was a good kid deep down, but he couldn't get himself out of the rut he'd fallen into. It was a wrong place, wrong time situation.

Well, he came to live with my family and me for his senior year, and we helped him turn it all around. He was allowed to stay in school, he passed all his classes, and he graduated. He went on to college, and in fact he's now a university professor—the kid who never wanted to show up for school, and now he's teaching it. Life is just funny sometimes. And it goes to show how a little investment, especially in an underdog, will pay off immensely in the end.

A little later on in life, my wife and I became acquainted with a couple of second-grade boys. They lived in their family homes, where there was abundant love but no male role models in sight. Their mothers, aunts, and grandmothers did exceptional jobs of raising these boys under less than ideal circumstances, and I would never discount the many sacrifices they undoubtedly made. But a boy needs a man in his life in some form or fashion; that is just a fact. He needs a father or an uncle after whom he can mold himself and in whom he can see how he is to navigate the world as a man. When that rudder is absent, the boy is essentially left out on a boat that's adrift at sea.

This was the state in which we found these boys. And while we didn't take them in as we had done with our nephews, I picked them up every other weekend until their high-school graduation. Sometimes we went to a park and played ball; sometimes it was a movie or a game or just hanging around at home, enjoying each other's company. It didn't really matter what we did; the purpose was to provide them with that presence they lacked and for them to learn through experience what it meant to be a boy and to grow into a man. In May of 2013, both of those boys—now young men—graduated from university. One is working on a PhD; the other joined the US Navy and is pursuing a career in law. I guess you could call them success stories, two examples of how investing in a child eventually pays off. I just call them family, and I feel fortunate that I was allowed to play some part in their success.

Get Out of Your Comfort Zone

By now it should be clear that education has been my life. In my career I have served (in Rochester and North Carolina) as: a teacher and a drug counselor at James Madison High School; an assistant principal at Eastside School in Jackson; an assistant principal and a principal at Gumberry High School, also in Jackson; a principal at Northampton County High School-West in Gaston; an associate superintendent of schools in Northampton County and then in Halifax County, where I was also a superintendent; and finally the chancellor of my alma mater, Elizabeth State City University in Elizabeth City.

In order to become an educator, of course I first underwent an education of my own—one that extended far into my adult years. As I progressed in my line of work, I required more knowledge and higher-level degrees in order to achieve each position. Along the way I earned a bachelor's of science degree in health and physical education at Elizabeth State

City University; a master's of science in administration from
Brockport State University in New York; an advanced degree
in administration from Virginia Polytechnic Institute; and a
doctorate of education, administration, and supervision from
NOVA Southeastern University in Fort Lauderdale, Florida.

Seems like a lot of work, doesn't it? That's because it was.
I put many, many hours into furthering my education. It took
up my free time, my time with family and friends, and a good
portion of my paychecks for a while. But in the end—and even
along the way—it was all worth it. Because there are few things
in life that will stay with you forever, and education is one of
them. Once you have a degree, no one can take that away from
you.

This was something I learned early on in life. My parents,
though they were not college educated themselves (in fact
their educations had stopped in grade school), urged me
toward going to university because they knew having a degree
would give me a leg up in the world and spur me on to those
bigger and better things all parents want for their children. I
always agreed with them, and as I neared the age when I would
apply to and attend college, I found myself becoming more
and more excited about the prospect. I pictured myself sitting
in classes with my fellow students, all of us nodding know-
ingly as a professor elucidated the finer points of some great
novel or mathematical equation. I would spend long nights
huddled over a pile of books at the library, making discoveries
and writing papers on topics I'd never even heard of before. It
would be four years of learning and amazement, and at the end

I would leave with a diploma in hand and a head full of knowledge that would propel me into the perfect job of my dreams.

Perhaps I was a bit optimistic. College can be all those things; there are certainly lively discussions in class from time to time, and you will spend many mornings, afternoons, and evenings in the library if you live on campus and have a roommate. (Who can think, much less study, with someone else hovering over them all the time?) But other than that, it's not at all like it is in the movies, as they say. It's a lot of drudgery and hard work; it's a long, drawn-out marathon with exams and all-nighters along the way instead of rest stops and water breaks.

Of course I didn't know this going in. When I got my letter of acceptance to Elizabeth State City University, I was nothing but thrilled, as were my parents, and my head was full of those dreams of academic erudition. As I packed all my meager belongings to cart off to campus with me since I'd had no experience like this before and no one to tell me what to bring and what to leave at home, I wondered what the food would be like at the dining hall, how long it would take me to walk from my dorm to my classes, and whether or not I should pledge a fraternity. I was giddy with excitement, about ready to burst at the seams if I didn't get to the school soon and jump right in. This was to be the start of my new life as a scholar and a respected man. After a lifetime so far of being a child, I was really looking forward to the change.

However, what I found when I arrived at Elizabeth City State was not at all what I had expected. The campus was beautiful, and my room was spacious enough that my assigned roommate and I could maneuver without bumping into one another, which was nice. My whole family came with me and helped me get the room set up and made sure I was settled in before they left. There were lots of hugs and kisses and some tears before we parted, and after they piled back into the car and headed off, I stood on the front steps of the dormitory for a long time, staring down the road even after I couldn't see them anymore. For the first time in my life, I was truly alone. I was on my own. And I was *terrified*.

From that moment on I was miserable. I wandered back into my room, found my way to the dining hall for dinner, and went to bed in a daze. The next morning I woke up and went to class, but it wasn't the magical experience I'd envisioned. I was surrounded by strangers who all seemed to know each other already, and none of them seemed to notice I existed.

I went back to my room, crawled into bed, and cried. And I did the same thing at the end of every day for the next two weeks. I was sad and lonely, just a dismal wreck. I didn't like being surrounded by people I didn't know (though of course it didn't occur to me that maybe I could introduce myself and get to know them). I missed my family terribly, and I wanted to go home. Of that much I was sure.

So I called my dad and told him so. I sobbed and begged him to come back and pick me up. I told him I'd made a big mistake, that college was not for me, that I couldn't take it one day longer. I would pack my bags and be waiting outside for him if he'd just agree to come get me.

And of course he didn't. After all the years he'd spent telling me that I needed to get an education and not end up working at a hard-labor, blue-collar job like he did, he was not about to let me give up after only a handful of days. Of course it was difficult, he told me. This was a new experience; I was in a situation I'd never had to be in before. It would take time for me to adjust, and I just had to hang on until I did.

When I hung up from that phone call, I was in a daze. I sat at my desk with my head in my hands, wondering what I would do—what I could do. I couldn't make it through another week at school. That much I knew. But I had to. What other choice did I have? Dad said I had to stay, so I had to stay. He wouldn't come to bring me home, and I couldn't afford any form of public transportation that might get me there. It was simply too far and too expensive.

So I continued to plod through my classes for the rest of that third week. I showed up, I listened distractedly to the lectures, I took halfhearted notes. Every meal I ate was tasteless, every night when I could return to my room and flop into bed an unbelievable relief. I tried, in some small way, to make things better for myself. I tried to bring back that optimism I'd felt before I'd arrived at Elizabeth City State University, back when I'd had no idea what college was really like. But it didn't work. Now that I'd seen it, now that I was living in it, I couldn't convince myself it was anything but hell on earth—one from which I had no chance of escaping.

At the end of the week, I called my father again and once more begged him to let me quit school and come home.

"I'll never fit in here," I told him in between sniffles and gulps. "I'm too much of a homebody. I don't have any friends, and the work is so hard, Dad...I'm gonna fail out, I just know it."

He was silent on the other end of the line for a while, so I knew he was thinking. Dad had always been a fair man, willing to listen to what my siblings and I had to say, even when we were small children, before he made any decisions. For a moment I had a glimmer of hope that he'd agree with me, that he'd get in the car, drive down to North Carolina, and bring me home, where I could—well, I didn't know. Get a job, maybe, or go to a closer school so I could still live with my parents while pursuing my studies. That would, I believed, make the whole thing a lot easier.

Alas, that was not what Dad had planned. "Willie," he told me, his voice gentle but firm, "you can come home at Thanksgiving. Not before then."

I was silent. But Thanksgiving was more than two months away. How would I survive for that long? It didn't seem possible. But there was no questioning his decision; as usual, my father's word was law—although that didn't stop me from calling him again with the same request the following week. And his response that time?

"Forget Thanksgiving. Now you can wait until Christmas to come home."

That was the last devastating blow. I knew not to ask or even complain again. I would be staying at school until December, no ifs, ands, or buts about it.

For the rest of that autumn, I continued trudging forward, attending my classes and trying to get the best grades I could. College was, understandably, more difficult than high school had been, but I had always been a good student and managed to bring in A's and B's on my exams and papers. That gave me some confidence and made being there just a tiny bit more bearable but not enough, really, to convince me that I should stay past the first semester. In the back of my mind, I was already planning to go home for winter break and never return to the university. My father wouldn't like it, I knew, but once I was back in Rochester, how could he force me to leave?

That was the thought that kept me going. I counted down the days until December 20, when school would let out. I kept my head down as I strode across campus from class to class, refusing to let anything around me that might have been good seep into my consciousness, even accidentally. Elizabeth City might have been a lovely place—and it was—but I didn't want to see anything good about it. All I wanted was to do my time and get out.

I was able to keep that up for a couple of weeks. And then one Tuesday I picked up my mail at the student center and found an envelope from my dad. I turned it over in my hands, double checking the return address. This was odd; he'd never sent me mail before, and I hadn't ever expected him to. He'd never been a letter writer, and he could call me on the phone whenever he wanted to. Needless to say, the appearance of this envelope made me very, very curious.

I went directly back to my room, dropped my books on my

desk, and sat on the bed. I looked at the envelope for a moment then slid my finger underneath the corner of the flap and tore it open. Inside was a greeting card. I slid it out carefully. It was thick and white, and a poem was printed on the front—Rudyard Kipling's "If." I read the whole thing slowly and then read it again. It was a letter of sorts from a father to a son, and the message was this: if you can be brave and righteous and keep moving forward, you will cease to be a boy; you will be a *man*. The idea immediately resonated with me, and I sat up a little straighter as I scanned the poem a third time. This time I heard my father's voice reciting it.

Finally I opened the card. Inside it my father had written a note to me in his small, neat handwriting: "I went into a store, saw this card, and knew it was for you. I hope it inspires you to keep going. Love, Dad."

And it did exactly that. I stood the card up on my desk and looked at it every morning when I got up then again before I turned in every night. Though it really was just a piece of paper with some ink on it, it was a symbol to me, a tangible sign of the faith and confidence my father had in me. It was also a reminder that I was no longer a high-school boy; I was a college-educated man now, and it was time for me to act like one. Once I was able to get that idea into my admittedly thick head, things got a lot better for me. The school routine became comfortable instead of bleak and repetitive; I continued to get good grades, but now I enjoyed learning. I was interested in the subjects I studied. All the hope I'd had for a scintillating and enlightening college experience suddenly came back to me, and with it came my motivation to succeed, which I had temporarily lost along the way. That mopey, depressed, scared young man I'd been for the first month or so of my college career—that hadn't been the real me. And all it took was knowing that my father had such confidence in me to bring me right back to my old self.

From that point on I really tried make the best of my time at the university. I kept my head up, and there was no more crying in my room at night. October flew by, then November, and before I knew it Thanksgiving had arrived, and I didn't even mind staying at school with some other students whose homes were too far away to travel to for just a weekend. For the next month I was too busy studying for and then taking final exams to think about anything else.

Then, finally, it was the week before Christmas. All my classes were wrapped up; it was all over except for finding out my final grades, which would be posted by the time my classmates and I returned from the two-week holiday break. In my dorm room I happily packed up the clothes and personal items I would need for the short trip from what had become my home away from home then I said good-bye to my friends and set out toward the train station and the four-hundred-mile ride to Rochester.

About nine hours later, when I arrived in New York, there were two feet of snow on the ground. I stood outside the train station, suitcase in hand, and zipped up my jacket, wishing I had a pair of boots to wear. North Carolina wasn't as year-round hot as the Florida of my childhood had been, but it didn't have winters like the northern states did, either. I had no use for heavy coats and snow boots down there, and so I hadn't brought them with me in the first place. All such gear of mine sat in the hall closet of my parents' house, gathering dust a mere fifteen minutes away from where I now stood.

The walk didn't take long, but by the time I rounded the corner onto my block, the tops of my tennis shoes were soaked through, and my toes were frozen. I walked with my head down, trying to keep the driving, icy wind off of my face, but I knew the route to my parents' house by heart; I didn't even have to see the house to know that I was nearing it. Finally I reached the pathway up to the front steps—or where the pathway would have been if it weren't covered in snow—and I raised my eyes, anxious to see some familiar sights after four long months. And they were all there: the two-story house, the bushes and trees in the yard, and warm lighting in every window.

But there was something new as well. At the top of the steps, a tall sheet of plywood leaned against a column of the porch, a message written on it in red paint: "WELCOME HOME!"

Tears immediately sprang to my eyes and turned to frost along my lashes. I reached up to wipe them away, and in that moment—standing on the walkway outside my childhood home, returning from my first semester of college, witnessing this sign of love and support from my family—I realized how far I had come. The card my dad had sent me back at the beginning of the school year popped into my head. Keep your head about you when others falter, it had said; trust yourself and pursue your dreams and take your losses and triumphs in stride. Since September I had learned to do every one of those things and more. I had learned to step outside my comfort zone, put myself in unfamiliar territory, and adapt to it as necessary. And thanks to all that, although I had left this place as a boy, I had now come back as a man.

It was one of the best feelings I've ever had in my life.

———

You could read that story about the inauspicious start of my life in higher education and think, *Well, that happens to most people.* And you would be right about that. Plenty of kids who go off to college are scared at first; while they might have been the big fish back in high school, they've now been thrown into a very big sea compared to their little ponds back home. And that's gonna hurt no matter what. Some are resilient enough to adapt right away, find their footing, and get on with things. For others, like me, it takes a little more time and encouragement. But in the end it *will* happen. All one needs is the fortitude to see it out.

That first Christmas when I went home, I was happy to be back there, but I was also happy that I had stuck it out at school. And to this day I'm so grateful to my father for not allowing me to leave the university and crawl back to Rochester as I'd wanted to do in the beginning. If I had, my life would have turned out very differently. I probably would not have earned a degree, much less four of them. I would not have achieved all the career accomplishments I'd set out for myself back then and along the way after that. And, most important, I would not have met my wife, whose path I crossed during that first semester—after I had decided to stay. We wouldn't have gotten married during our junior year, and we wouldn't have our three wonderful children and our six cherished grandchildren. Every minute of this life I've had has been a blessing, and I never would have experienced any of it if I hadn't learned the hard way the most important lesson of all: being comfortable is easy; it takes real courage to step out into the unknown and face what's waiting for you.

Parting Thoughts

Everyone thinks they've had an interesting life and that their story deserves to be told—that something they have gone through could serve as inspiration, whether negative or positive, to someone else who might be struggling with a similar issue. I must feel this way as well, to some degree, or I wouldn't have written this book, right?

But that doesn't mean I think my life has been better than anyone else's. Yes, I have achieved some things that I think are great. I'm proud of them; I am proud of myself and what I have managed to overcome and accomplish in my time on this Earth so far. Some of it has been easy, some of it not so much. But that, too, is life. As I said at the beginning of this book, we've all been through our own trials, and we've seen some good times too. Into every life a little rain must fall; isn't that the way the saying goes? But eventually the storm passes, and in its wake it leaves brilliant sunshine and fields full of beautiful wildflowers. In other words you've got to take the bad if you want to get to the good.

This is universal, as is the advice I've tried to impart with the writing I've done here. I don't purport to be an expert on how to live well, but I believe I have managed to do so, for the most part, thanks to these tools I have learned to use throughout my life. Some of them I have found on my own through personal experience; some my parents passed on to me; some I have borrowed from mentors, colleagues, and loved ones. But no matter what their origins, they have all worked toward one purpose: bringing me closer and closer to the places I wanted to be, whether those existed on the physical, emotional, or spiritual plane. Sometimes my goal was to earn a specific degree or to be hired for a particular job. Sometimes it was to spend as much time as possible with my children, to enjoy their company and nurture and teach them as they grew. And all the time I strive to be the best husband, father, brother, son, friend, boss, or employee I can be. No matter what role I am fulfilling, I am giving it my all. Because if I don't do my best, what's the point in doing anything?

Having said that, I want to note that I recognize how much easier said than done that is. It's great to read motivational books that tell you to just go out there and grab what you want, that whatever you wish to possess is yours for the taking if only you reach far or high enough. Sometimes this is true. There are occasions, rare though they are, when everything seems to come easily. We have to work toward what we want but not too hard; we have to get out there and go for it, but the journey is more like a hop, skip, and a jump than a marathon we have to run. These times are blessed for sure. Take them in, revel in them, and celebrate the successes that seem to fall into your lap. Just because you didn't have to sweat for them, that doesn't mean they hold no value. A good thing is a good thing is a good thing, and no good thing in your life should be turned away.

However, you must also be prepared for times that are not so easy because these are what you will experience the most. This sounds terrible, doesn't it? Like your time on this planet will just be one long torture session, one disappointment and hardship after another with possible—not guaranteed—respites of happiness along the way. If that's how you view working for something you want then I wish you luck, but I'm not sure any of the advice I've imparted here will help. To get anywhere in life, you must have the drive to do so; you have to want it enough that you're willing to get up out of your chair and do something about it. Whether this means enrolling in school for that degree you never earned, requesting your boss give you that overdue raise, or finally asking the girl of your dreams to be your wife, none of it will happen if you don't make it happen. As the poet once said, and I paraphrase, you are the master of your fate; you are the captain of your soul. No one is responsible for creating yourself as a person but you.

Most of all, you are the only person who can fill your toolbox as you go along. Take the implements I've offered you in this book and carry them with you and use them well. But also learn to spot your own new tools along the way. You will find them in obvious places—with your friends and family, at your job, in the education I hope you will pursue—and in areas that might surprise you as well, such as within yourself.

You are your first, best, and last resource; never forget that. When nothing around you seems to work, only you can give it a jumpstart and get it going again.

Last, and certainly not the least, remember to pass on what you have learned to those who come after you. Your children, your students, whomever you are responsible for teaching the ways of the world to, open your toolbox to them. Share the wisdom you've culled from every source in your life. Further, teach them *how* to use these tools for themselves. Because it's in that passing on of the torch, so to speak, that we reach our highest calling. You can have all the success and knowledge in the world, but if you keep them to yourself, what good are they? They'll be merely ideas with no reason to exist. No, a tool fulfills its purpose in its use, so take yours out and exercise them often—for you and for the people around you. Only then will you be able to find success in whatever form it happens to take for you. And I wish you luck on this journey.

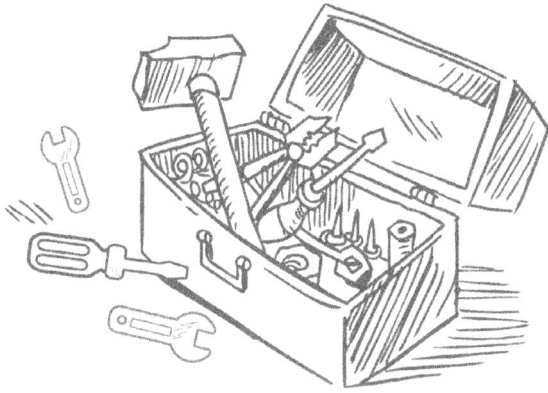